THE RESTORED GOSPEL AND THE BOOK OF GENESIS

THE RESTORED
GOSPEL AND THE
BOOK OF GENESIS

KENT P. JACKSON

DESERET
BOOK

SALT LAKE CITY, UTAH

Library of Congress Cataloging-in-Publication Data

Jackson, Kent P.
   The restored gospel and the book of Genesis / Kent P. Jackson.
      p.   cm.
   Includes bibliographical references and index.
   ISBN 1–57008–727-X
   1. Bible. O.T. Genesis English—Versions—Smith. 2. Bible. O.T. Genesis—Commentaries. I. Title.

BX8630 .J33 2001
222.'1106'088283—dc21   2001004761

Printed in the United States of America   18961-6868
R. R. Donnelley and Sons, Crawfordsville, IN

10   9   8   7   6   5   4   3   2   1

CONTENTS

PREFACE

T HIS BOOK IS AN EXPLORATION of Genesis in the bright light of the latter-day restoration of the gospel. It does not cover all the people, events, and teachings of Genesis, only those for which modern revelation through the Prophet Joseph Smith has provided new context, clarification, or understanding.

We do not have all the answers to the questions that naturally arise from our reading of scripture, and this is probably more true with regard to Genesis than any other book. But it is also true that modern revelation provides the keys for our understanding and teaches us clearly those things that matter most. My desire in this volume has been to show what the questions are and what the sources are for dealing with those questions. The answers I have proposed are my own interpretations. It has been my intent that they be consistent with what the Lord has revealed, but I encourage readers to go beyond my conclusions to the true sources themselves—the standard works of the Church and the inspired teachings of the Lord's prophets.

I would like to thank my generous colleagues and student

research assistants at Brigham Young University who read chapters of this book and provided recommendations for its improvement. And I am grateful to my wife, Nancy, whose careful readings yielded much-appreciated suggestions.

INTRODUCTION

B EGINNING WITH THE FIRST VISION, the latter-day restoration of the gospel has set in motion a significant interaction between new revelation and the Bible. In some cases that interaction has been a reaffirmation of the Bible's integrity and the truth of its history and teachings. One of the Restoration's purposes has been to "prov[e] to the world that the holy scriptures are true" (D&C 20:11; cf. 1 Ne. 13:39). Modern revelation has served to sustain, defend, and "establish the truth" of the Bible by providing additional witnesses to its history and teachings (1 Ne. 13:40).

In other cases, the interaction of the Restoration with the Bible has been to show that there is much truth that has been lost since the time of its original writers. The scriptures of the Restoration, as an angel told the Book of Mormon prophet Nephi, would "make known the plain and precious things which have been taken away." Above all, modern revelation would "make known to all kindreds, tongues, and people, that the Lamb of God is the Son of the Eternal Father, and the Savior

1

of the world; and that all men must come unto him, or they cannot be saved" (1 Ne. 13:40).

The contributions of modern revelation to our understanding of Genesis come from several sources. It is in Genesis that the Joseph Smith Translation's largest and most significant insertions are found, with page after page of new material unknown from any other source. To those revelations are added important contributions from the Book of Mormon, the Doctrine and Covenants, the book of Abraham, and Joseph Smith's sermons and writings. Together they reveal fundamental doctrines that set apart our religion from the rest of Christianity—doctrines that are at the very heart of the Latter-day Saint faith.

This volume attempts to bring together the book of Genesis, passed down through the centuries from antiquity, with sources revealed in the latter days that flood it with truth and light. We see first how modern revelation teaches us of the identity of Jehovah—the God of the Old Testament. We learn how his acts of creation, revelation, and atonement have been manifested from before the world to our own time. We are reminded that it is through latter-day revelation that we come to know him better than we could if we had only the Bible as our guide (chapter 1). We learn how the Latter-day Saint view of the Bible has caused some of our fellow Christians to question our belief in it. We believe, indeed, that it has not been transmitted to us in its ancient purity, and we believe in other scripture in addition to the Bible. Yet we see how modern revelation does not distract us from our belief in the Bible but serves to confirm to us its value and its truth (chapter 2). We learn what the Joseph Smith Translation of the Bible is, how we obtained it, what it does, and how it serves as a witness both for Christ and his work and for the prophetic ministry of

Joseph Smith (chapter 3). We learn also what the Old
Testament is—a great collection of books that include the writings of prophets, historians, and poets who bore testimony of
Jehovah anciently and continue through their words to reach
out to us today (chapter 4).

Modern revelation does not give us all the answers to difficult Bible questions, but it does give us tools that we need as
we approach those questions. We discuss the authorship of
Genesis and see what the restored gospel teaches on that matter. Moses is our best choice as the author, but many intriguing
questions remain (chapter 5). Similarly, the first lesson we learn
about the Creation is that there are many things about it we do
not know and probably will not know until the Millennium. We
attempt to separate things of which we can be certain from
those for which we need further thought and revelation. We see
how scripture and the principles of science are not opponents
but complementary revelations of God's creative work (chapter
6). We learn how modern revelation reaffirms the reality of
Adam and Eve. Even though we do not know all the answers
about how they were created, we do know of their uniqueness
among God's creations and of their role in his divine plan
(chapter 7). The restored gospel teaches us of the reality of the
Fall. We learn what the circumstances were in the Garden of
Eden and how the Fall brought consequences that we still experience today. We see that the Fall was part of God's grand
design for his children and how the atonement of Jesus Christ
overcomes its effects and enables us to return to our Heavenly
Father (chapter 8).

One of the most dramatic revelations of new text in the
Joseph Smith Translation of the Bible focuses on the years
between the fall of Adam and the translation of the City of
Enoch. We see the expanding influence of Satan in the world

as humanity moved on the course that led eventually to the Flood and the destruction of almost all humankind. Yet we see that in those same days, the kingdom of God was growing, culminating in the removal of Enoch and his sanctified city from the earth. In these revelations we learn the principles of Zion that apply in all generations, including our own (chapter 9).

Modern revelation teaches us more about some Bible characters than does the Bible itself. Enoch and Melchizedek are obvious examples. Among other things, we learn that Melchizedek presided over a community that was translated, as Enoch's city had been previously. We learn that the ancient patriarchs had the gospel and taught and administered it through priesthood and covenants, looking forward to the mortal ministry of Jesus Christ (chapter 10). We come to understand the Abrahamic covenant, with its promises of land, posterity, and priesthood and with its calling to bless the world through service and temple ordinances (chapter 11).

The Restoration gives us perspective for understanding the accounts of Israel's ancestors. Through the lives of the matriarchs and patriarchs whose descendants became God's covenant people, we are reminded of our own challenges in facing life's realities. Through the Restoration we are reminded also of our potential to do great things in the world and to become celestial families in the eternities (chapter 12). Sacred events recounted in Genesis—a ladder ascending into heaven and a prophet wrestling for a blessing—are understood through modern revelation in ways not possible from the Bible alone. Our temples provide the context for these and other transcendent experiences recorded in the Old Testament (chapter 13). Joseph was a type both of Christ and of Joseph's own latter-day descendants. Called to a special mission, he brought salvation to his family by providing for their safety and blessing. Modern revelation helps us see his life as part of God's plan for his covenant people, a foreshadowing of what is taking place today as the Lord gathers again his people to the covenant promises he made to their ancient progenitors (chapter 14).

Genesis is a precious treasure, rich in purpose and content. The knowledge we gain through the restored gospel infuses it with light and makes its truths ever more "plain" and "precious" than before (1 Ne. 13:40).

1

JEHOVAH, LORD OF HEAVEN AND EARTH

THE DIVINE NAME THAT IS WRITTEN "the LORD" in the King James translation of the Bible is spelled with four letters in Hebrew: *y h w h*. It was probably pronounced *Yahweh* in ancient times,[1] with some other variant pronunciations.[2] The form of the name familiar to English speakers is *Jehovah,* with spelling and pronunciation established during the 1500s.[3] Yahweh is God's name in the Old Testament, the name by which he was called by believers and nonbelievers alike. The name appears more than five thousand times in the Hebrew Bible—in poetry, prophecy, and in common conversation—and it is attested also in numerous nonbiblical Hebrew inscriptions.[4] This is the name that Moses, David, Isaiah, Jeremiah, and undoubtedly Lehi and Nephi used with reference to their God, the God of Israel.

Most Hebrew names, like ancient Semitic names in general, had meanings that could be understood by native speakers. Names almost always formed complete sentences that praised a quality or a great act of God or asked for a blessing. For example, *Jonathan* means "Yahweh Has Given," *Jeremiah* means "May Yahweh Lift (Me) Up," *Elijah* means "Yahweh Is (My)

God," and *Daniel* means "God Is My Judge." Usually a name of God is part of the person's name, as with *Jo-*, *-iah*, and *-jah* (Yahweh), and *El-* and *-el* (God) in the examples above.[5]

Like other names, the name *Yahweh* creates a sentence. It is a conjugation of the archaic verb *hwy* (biblical Hebrew *hyh*), "to be." The best explanation seems to be that it is in a causative form and means something like "He Causes to Be" or "He Causes to Exist." The tense is one of continuous duration, suggesting that the Creator maintains and sustains as well as causes. Unlike most ancient Hebrew names, there is no deity name in this one, undoubtedly because the bearer of the name himself is the Divine One. And unlike many names, there is no object specified. The unstated but implied object is all-inclusive: Yahweh is the creator and sustainer of *all* things.[6]

After the Old Testament period ended, when prophecy had ceased and the Jews viewed themselves as more distant from God than their ancestors had been, the people adopted a custom, based perhaps on an exaggerated reading of Exodus 20:7, that it was blasphemous to pronounce God's name. They used substitute words in place of *Yahweh.* As they read the Hebrew manuscripts of the Bible, when they came upon God's name they substituted in its place the word *'ădōnāy,* "my Lord(s)." Greek-speaking Jewish translators in the third century before Christ solved the problem by replacing the divine name with the common Greek noun *kýrios,* "Lord." By New Testament times these substitutions were firmly in place in Jewish culture. Most modern translations have continued the custom. In the King James translation, whenever God's name *Yahweh* appears in the text, the translators have rendered it as "the LORD." Capital letters are used to set the divine name apart from the common English noun *lord,* which means *master.*

One of the many great blessings of the restoration of the

gospel is the understanding it has brought into the world concerning the mission of Jehovah—the Lord Jesus Christ. The
Book of Mormon, the Doctrine and Covenants, the Pearl of
Great Price, and the sermons and writings of the Prophet
Joseph Smith not only provide a powerful witness to Christ's
existence but also bless the world with a knowledge of who he
is, what his gospel plan entails, and what our relationship is
and should be to him. With these latter-day witnesses and
those of the Old and New Testaments, we know that Christ
lives and also what it means to us that he lives.

The mortal Jesus was no ordinary Jewish carpenter from
Galilee. Before his earthly birth, he was divine and ruled in
glory under his Father. Abraham saw Christ in premortal glory
and testified that he was "like unto God" (Abr. 3:22–24) or, as
Paul wrote, "equal with God" (Philip. 2:6). Jesus himself, in
praying to his Father, said, "And now, O Father, glorify thou me
with thine own self with the glory which I had with thee before
the world was" (John 17:5). Into the hands of him who became
his Only Begotten in the flesh, the Father has given all power
and authority. He is "the brightness of [the Father's] glory, and
the express image of his person" (Heb. 1:3). The divine acts of
creating worlds without number, governing this earth and
countless others like it, revealing the divine will to prophets,
and atoning for the sins of God's children were part of the mission of Jesus Christ—Jehovah—who was, as King Benjamin
taught, "the Lord Omnipotent who reigneth, who was, and is
from all eternity to all eternity" (Mosiah 3:5).

A correct understanding of Jesus Christ must include a
knowledge of the broad range of his eternal ministry. The scriptures teach us that Christ is the *Creator,* the *Revealer,* and the
Redeemer.

CREATOR

Both ancient and modern scriptures testify that Christ was the Creator. To Joseph Smith he said, "Thus saith the Lord your God, even Jesus Christ, the Great I AM, Alpha and Omega. . . . I am the same which spake, and the world was made, and all things came by me" (D&C 38:1–3). John wrote, "All things were made by him; and without him was not any thing made that was made" (John 1:3). Paul wrote that by Christ "were all things created, that are in heaven, and that are in earth, visible and invisible, . . . all things were created by him, and for him" (Col. 1:16). King Benjamin called Christ "the Creator of all things from the beginning" (Mosiah 3:8).

Moses gained a clear view of the role of Christ in the Creation while he was shown God's work in a glorious vision. The Lord said: "By the word of my power, have I created them, which is mine Only Begotten Son, who is full of grace and truth. And worlds without number have I created; and I also created them for mine own purpose; and by the Son I created them, which is mine Only Begotten" (Moses 1:32–33; cf. Heb. 1:2).

Jehovah continues to preside over his creations: He "uphold[s] all things by the word of his power" (Heb. 1:3), and the light that emanates from him fills "the immensity of space," "giveth life to all things," and governs all creation (D&C 88:12–13; see also vv. 7–11). Indeed, as his name indicates, "He Causes to Exist," and he maintains all things in their existence.

REVEALER

Jesus Christ, the God of ancient and modern Israel, has spoken with his prophets since the beginning of time. President

Joseph Fielding Smith taught: "All revelation since the fall has come through Jesus Christ, who is the Jehovah of the Old Testament. In all of the scriptures, where God is mentioned and where he has appeared, it was Jehovah who talked with Abraham, with Noah, Enoch, Moses and all the prophets. He is the God of Israel, the Holy One of Israel."[7] The Book of Mormon also teaches this doctrine, and it was expressed by the Lord himself when he appeared to Lehi's children after his resurrection: "I am he that gave the law, and I am he who covenanted with my people Israel" (3 Ne. 15:5; see also 1 Ne. 19:7–10, 13–14; 3 Ne. 11:14; 15:8). In modern times Christ has also revealed himself as Jehovah: "Listen to the voice of Jesus Christ, your Redeemer, the Great I AM" (D&C 29:1; see also 38:1; 39:1).

REDEEMER

Jehovah's ministry was not limited to his acts of creation, his governing of the worlds, or his communication with prophets. As the Word of God, the embodiment of the Father's will, he had a divine mission, which included coming to earth as a mortal, being tested to a greater degree than anyone else, overcoming every trial and temptation without committing sin, and suffering for the sins of the world. His coming to earth in the humblest of circumstances—born in a stable to a poor family far from home—disguised his divine identity and the mission for which he was sent. Yet it was only under such lowly circumstances that his work could have been done, for he needed to descend below all things (see D&C 88:6). As a children's Christmas hymn teaches so beautifully,

> He came down to earth from heaven,
> Who is God and Lord of all,

And His shelter was a stable
And his cradle was a stall;
With the poor, and mean, and lowly,
Lived on earth our Saviour holy.[8]

Paul knew and understood the nature of the condescension of Jehovah: Jesus "made himself of no reputation, and took upon him the form of a servant, and was made in the likeness of men: And being found in fashion as a man, he humbled himself" (Philip. 2:7–8). Indeed, Jesus "la[id] his glory by" when he came to earth.[9] He became mortal, like us, so he could more fully touch our lives: "Wherefore in all things it behoved him to be made like unto his brethren, that he might be a merciful and faithful high priest in things pertaining to God, to make reconciliation for the sins of the people. For in that he himself hath suffered being tempted, he is able to succour them that are tempted" (Heb. 2:17–18). "For we have not an high priest which cannot be touched with the feeling of our infirmities; but was in all points tempted like as we are, yet without sin" (Heb. 4:15). One reason for his descending from his divine throne to become as we are was to establish the pattern for us to follow. Jehovah became one of us so he could demonstrate that we can indeed keep the commandments and overcome the trials and temptations of life. It is of immeasurable worth to the millions who have experienced sorrow in their mortal existence to know that there is one who has sorrowed more. And those who have suffered trials and temptations can know that there is one who not only has overcome such adversity but who empathizes with those who are still struggling to learn how.

For He is our childhood's pattern,
Day by day like us He grew:
He was little, weak, and helpless,

Tears and smiles like us He knew;
And He feeleth for our sadness,
And He shareth in our gladness.[10]

But Christ's mortality entailed much more than setting a good example. It included his atoning suffering—suffering that is beyond human comprehension. He descended below *all* things, suffered more than we can suffer, and sorrowed more than we can sorrow. And all this was done for others, an expression of his incomparable grace, the greatest of his many divine attributes. Paul bore witness: "He humbled himself, and became obedient unto death, even the death of the cross" (Philip. 2:8). As we ponder Jesus' suffering in our behalf, let us not forget who he is. This is Jehovah, Almighty God himself, who descended from his throne of glory, submitted himself to mortality, suffered, and died—for us.

Jesus' atonement, the ultimate act of sacrifice and servitude, was also his greatest triumph. In carrying out this labor of supreme love he demonstrated for all what greatness really means. His atonement shows the pettiness of our own vain delusions of grandeur and our obsession with status and its symbols. All definitions of worth must be measured against the example of Christ. Our man-made scales do not measure real value; instead, they pervert it. When James and John and their mother approached the Master with requests for status and position in the hereafter, he gently taught them the error of the world's understanding of such things. From him they learned that real greatness comes not in rank but in service: "Ye know that the princes of the Gentiles exercise dominion over them, and they that are great exercise authority upon them. But it shall not be so among you: but whosoever will be great among you, let him be your *minister*; and whosoever will be chief among you, let him be your *servant:* even as the Son of man came not to be ministered unto, but to minister, and to give his life a ransom for many" (Matt. 20:25–28; emphasis added).

Jesus knew better than anyone else the true definition of greatness, for he who was greatest of all had descended to the lowest, so that when he returned to his rightful place of glory, he could take others—some of *us*—with him. When Jesus met with his disciples at the Last Supper, he told them: "In my Father's house are many mansions. . . . I go to prepare a place for you. And if I go and prepare a place for you, I will come again, and receive you unto myself; that where I am, there ye may be also" (John 14:2–3). Too often when we read these words, we envision Jesus going ahead to our new celestial house, straightening the furniture, dusting off the tables, and readying the place for our arrival. But where did he really go to "prepare a place" for us, and what were the preparations that had to be made? The answer is found in a revelation to Joseph Smith: "I, God, have suffered these things for all, that they might not suffer if they would repent; but if they would not repent they must suffer even as I; which suffering caused myself, even God, the greatest of all, to tremble because of pain, and to bleed at every pore, and to suffer both body and spirit— and would that I might not drink the bitter cup, and shrink— nevertheless, glory be to the Father, and I partook and finished my preparations unto the children of men" (D&C 19:16–19).

Indeed, to prepare a place for us, our Savior went ahead to Gethsemane and Golgotha, descended below all things, and suffered and died in our behalf. Only then did he return to the presence of the Father. Do we follow him in the torturous, descending path that he took? No. His atonement created a shortcut so we would not have to follow him in his sufferings, if we repent. Christ gave us a straight and direct route to the mansion that he promised us, the mansion that he prepared at a price that we cannot even imagine. But he would not have it otherwise. His love and grace are such that he would do this, as he said, so "that where I am, there ye may be also" (John 14:3), or, as Joseph Smith paraphrased, so "that the exaltation that I receive you may receive also."[11]

Jesus did return to his place of glory. He who was called in mortality the sacrificial "Lamb of God" is now in eternity the "KING OF KINGS, AND LORD OF LORDS" (Rev. 19:16). But even with his return to glory he has not yet ceased his work, for we are not yet there with him. His eternal mission, like that of his Father, is to bring to pass our "immortality and eternal life" (Moses 1:39). To accomplish this, his gospel plan helps us gain qualities that reflect his divine nature, and obedience to his laws and ordinances helps us overcome our weaknesses and become more like him. But the preeminent ingredient of our salvation is and always will be his grace.

Perhaps Jesus' parable of the lost sheep gives us a glimpse into the depth of the love that motivates him: his work is not finished until every effort has been expended to save each individual soul who will choose to follow him (see Luke 15:1–7; see also vv. 8–10). "Thus saith the Lord God; Behold, I, even I, will both search my sheep, and seek them out. . . . So will I seek out my sheep, and will deliver them out of all places where they have been scattered in the cloudy and dark day" (Ezek. 34:11–12). Some of the lost sheep will follow readily; others may need more time, more care, and more prodding from the divine Shepherd. But his atoning suffering has already shown that he considers no price too much to pay for our souls. Those who do respond to his voice, who cast aside the things of the world and come unto him, will receive his gentle invitation to join him in his Father's kingdom.

And our eyes at last shall see Him,
Through His own redeeming love;
For that Child so dear and gentle
Is our Lord in heaven above;
And He leads His children on
To the place where He is gone.

Not to that poor lowly stable,
With the oxen standing by,
We shall see Him, but in heaven,
Set at God's right hand on high;
When like stars His children crowned,
All in white shall wait around.[12]

Christ's beginnings are not to be found in a stable in a Palestinian village. He came from glory and has returned to glory. The place he has prepared for us—prepared through his atoning sacrifice—is a place of glory in the presence of the Father. Those who are faithful will inherit there "all that [the] Father hath" (D&C 84:38) and will forever rejoice in the blessings made possible through the ministry of the great Jehovah, our Lord Jesus Christ (see D&C 78:17–22).

Notes

1. David Noel Freedman and M. P. O'Connor, "*YHWH,*" in *Theological Dictionary of the Old Testament,* ed. G. Johannes Botterweck and Helmer Ringgren, trans. David E. Green (Grand Rapids, Mich.: Eerdmans, 1986), 5:500–521.

2. Perhaps including *Yah, Yaw,* and *Yahu.*

3. The earliest attestation of *Jehovah* in English is in William Tyndale's 1530 publication of the Pentateuch. See David Daniell, *William Tyndale: A Biography* (New Haven and London: Yale University Press, 1994), 284–85. See "Jehovah" in Tyndale's "A Table Expounding Certain Words," following Genesis in his 1530 Pentateuch; David Daniell, ed.,

Tyndale's Old Testament: Being the Pentateuch of 1530, Joshua to 2 Chronicles of 1537, and Jonah, Translated by William Tyndale (New Haven and London: Yale University Press, 1992), 82.

4. See G. I. Davies, *Ancient Hebrew Inscriptions: Corpus and Concordance* (Cambridge: Cambridge University Press, 1991), 366–67.

5. Because the King James translation substitutes *the* LORD for *Yahweh,* the more common translations for these names would be "The Lord Has Given," "May the Lord Lift (Me) Up," and "The Lord Is (My) God."

6. When Moses asked the Lord concerning his name, "God said unto Moses, I AM THAT I AM" (Ex. 3:14). *I AM* translates the Hebrew *'ehyeh* and is grammatically equivalent to *Yahweh. Yahweh* is the third-person form ("He Causes to Be"), whereas *'ehyeh,* what the Lord calls himself, is the first-person form ("I Cause to Be").

7. Joseph Fielding Smith, *Doctrines of Salvation,* comp. Bruce R. McConkie, 3 vols. (Salt Lake City: Bookcraft, 1954–56), 1:27.

8. Cecil Frances Alexander, "Once in Royal David's City," verse 2, in *A Treasury of Christmas Songs and Carols,* 2d ed., ed. Henry W. Simon (Boston: Houghton Mifflin, 1955), 186–87.

9. "Hark! The Herald Angels Sing," *Hymns of the Church of Jesus Christ of Latter-day Saints* (Salt Lake City: The Church of Jesus Christ of Latter-day Saints, 1985), no. 209, verse 2.

10. Alexander, "Once in Royal David's City," verse 4.

11. Andrew F. Ehat and Lyndon W. Cook, eds., *The Words of Joseph Smith: The Contemporary Accounts of the Nauvoo Discourses of the Prophet Joseph* (Provo, Utah: Religious Studies Center, Brigham Young University, 1980), 371.

12. Alexander, "Once in Royal David's City," verses 5 and 6.

2

Do We Believe in the Bible?

LATTER-DAY SAINTS BELIEVE IN THE BIBLE. We love it, and we believe its teachings. It holds a special place in our religion that cannot be filled by any other book. On the day the Church was organized, the Lord affirmed its truthfulness (see D&C 20:11), and the Book of Mormon itself bears testimony of the Bible and commits us to it (see 1 Ne. 13:20–23; 2 Ne. 29:2–13). With many other Christians, we have faith that the Bible's ancient writers were inspired, and we reject the trends in modern society that devalue it and its teachings. In many circles today, the Bible has been removed from the position of honor that it once held. Its history has been explained away as myth, the divine perspective of its authors has been viewed as primitive, and the moral standard it has held up to the world for almost two thousand years has been rejected as archaic and oppressive. We can be grateful for the many good people who have held fast to this book, and we join with them in expressing our thanks to God for it.

Why, then, do some think that Latter-day Saints do not accept the Bible? The reason is that we have significant beliefs regarding it that are very different from those of other Christians.

First, unlike many Bible-believing Christians, we maintain that the Bible did not arrive in the modern world in a pure state. Early in the Book of Mormon, the prophet Nephi wrote concerning the time of the early apostles and prophesied of a "great and abominable church," whose founder would be the devil. That church, consisting of apostate influences within early Christianity, would remove things "which are plain and most precious" both from the scriptures as well as from the gospel itself. The Bible would not go forth to the world until it had been corrupted "through the hands of the great and abominable church," leaving it less pure and reliable than it had been when it was first written (1 Ne. 13:4–6, 20–29).[1] Joseph Smith wrote, "Many important points, touching the salvation of man, had been taken from the Bible, or lost before it was compiled."[2] He stated, "[There are] many things in the Bible which do not, as they now stand, accord with the revelation of the Holy Ghost to me."[3] And he believed in the Bible "as it ought to be, as it came from the pen of the original writers."[4] But "ignorant translators, careless transcribers, or designing and corrupt priests have committed many errors."[5] Thus, "We believe the Bible to be the word of God as far as it is translated correctly" (A of F 8), with "translated" presumably including the entire process of transmission from original manuscripts to modern-language texts.

The second reason some claim we do not believe in the Bible is that we do not think it contains the totality of God's revelation to humankind. Although this idea is nowhere to be found in the Bible itself and actually contradicts the biblical precedent of God's calling prophets to provide current revelation to his people, many Christians think that believing in the

Bible means believing there can be no sacred scripture outside its covers. But because of the Restoration, Latter-day Saints believe otherwise. The Lord brought forth more scripture through the Prophet Joseph Smith than through any other prophet, ancient or modern. The Book of Mormon, the Doctrine and Covenants, and the Pearl of Great Price encompass 886 pages of new scriptural material.[6] We also have the Joseph Smith Translation of the Bible, the sermons and writings of the Prophet and his successors, and the ongoing inspired practices of the Lord's Church. The Restoration brought a flood of new knowledge that clarifies, adds to, substantiates, builds upon, and confirms what we know from the Bible. Thus when we read it, we do so in the light of the Restoration.

A PROPHETIC PRECEDENT

Joseph Smith was a restorer and revealer of scripture who loved the Bible and was a serious student of it. Indeed, his efforts to study and know it well constitute one of the keys of the Restoration. Over the years he learned the Bible so well that he could quote or paraphrase scores of passages without looking at his text. His speeches were punctuated with biblical lessons and biblical examples, showing not only a knowledge of the Bible itself but also a profound understanding of its doctrines.[7]

The Prophet knew that a mastery of the scriptures cannot come without paying the price of serious study. For example, in his personal journals during 1835–36, he frequently recorded his efforts to learn Hebrew so he could understand the Old Testament better.[8] Three important results of his Bible study make significant contributions to the Restoration.

First, the Joseph Smith Translation—the Prophet's inspired

revision of the Bible—is a direct result of several years of work and inspiration as he fulfilled his calling to provide a more correct translation for the Church. From this inspired enterprise we have Selections from the Book of Moses and Joseph Smith–Matthew in the Pearl of Great Price, and we have hundreds of other significant changes and additions, most of which are now included in the footnotes of the Church's 1979 publication of the English-language Bible.

Second, several of the revelations contained in the Doctrine and Covenants came as a result of questions raised in the Prophet's mind while he was engaged in the New Translation. Sections 76, 77, and 91 are obvious examples, but it is likely that many others had their origin in this same process, either directly or indirectly.

Third, to a great extent, it was in the process of his inspired study of the Bible that the Prophet gained much of his understanding of the gospel. And when he taught out of the Bible, he passed his knowledge on to others. From his recorded sermons, we can see that a significant portion of his public and private teaching consisted in expounding on Bible passages.[9] It was in these Bible-based sermons and teaching moments that he transmitted much of his revealed knowledge to the Church. We are heirs to what was revealed to him as he used the Bible as a springboard to revelation.

But the content of the Prophet's teaching was not the Bible. Rather, it was the heavenly enlightenment he received through his study of it. Indeed, the Bible was not the source for his theology; revelation from God was. It is clear from Joseph Smith's own words that he knew that what had been revealed to him was a surer source of knowledge than what he found printed on the page. This assertion may seem strange to those who do not share the testimony of the divinity of his calling, but those who recognize him as God's prophet—sent to restore truth in its purity for the last days—understand that the light and knowledge that was revealed to him is the standard against which *all* other religious ideas, traditions, or texts are to be judged—including the Bible. "God may correct the scripture by me if he choose," the Prophet taught.[10] Concerning the Bible he said, "I have the oldest book in the world and the Holy Ghost. I thank God for the old book, but more for the Holy Ghost."[11] Through the Prophet's inspired words as he discussed or taught from passages of the Bible, we can see the ancient scriptures in a new light and understand them in ways that would be impossible without divine tutoring. Joseph Smith, the great seer, had the capacity to see on Bible pages things not visible to the natural eye. This was possible because the Spirit that animated his interpretive powers was the same that had revealed the words originally through his ancient prophetic colleagues.

MODERN REVELATION

Though we love and use the Bible, we go first to the revelations of Joseph Smith to find answers to gospel questions. We should, in the language of President Ezra Taft Benson, "quote liberally from the words of the Lord to our dispensation," so that we will have guidance "from the Lord himself."[12]

Sometimes, well-meaning Latter-day Saints try to obtain an understanding of doctrinal issues by searching ancient prophecies—such as Isaiah or the book of Revelation—rather than modern scripture. Although on the surface this practice may seem appropriate or, at worst, harmless, there are at least three important reasons why we should focus on what the Lord has revealed in our own time to understand doctrine and to interpret the writings of the Bible.

First, much of the Bible, and most of biblical prophecy, is written in highly literary poetry, a fact not easily observed in the King James translation. Metaphor, the figurative language that is the primary tool in these writings, is understood completely only when the reader is part of the same cultural, linguistic, historical, geographical, and ideological world as the writer. Nephi pointed out this truth when he noted that he, a native Jerusalemite, could understand the prophetic writings but his children could not, they having been raised in a different culture and in a different land (see 2 Ne. 25:5–6). Perhaps that is what he meant when he spoke of knowing "the manner of prophesying among the Jews" (2 Ne. 25:1). Generally speaking, biblical prophecy was not intended to be difficult, but for most modern readers it is, because of a lack of familiarity with its literary style and the foreign world from which it came. These factors cause the Bible to be highly susceptible to misunderstanding, and too frequently this misunderstanding results in subjective interpretations.

In contrast, modern revelation has today's world as its cultural backdrop,[13] and thus it is, for the most part, clear and easily comprehended. It was revealed for our time, and we can understand it.

Second, the Bible has arrived in our day in a state of less than perfect preservation, as we have already seen.

Third, the most important reason for obtaining our gospel knowledge from modern revelation is doctrinal in nature. The Lord proclaimed to Joseph Smith, "This generation shall have my word through you" (D&C 5:10). A careful pondering of this brief statement should tell us we are to obtain God's word first from the revelations of Joseph Smith and his successors in the presidency of the Church. President Marion G. Romney, in a 1981 First Presidency editorial in the *Ensign,* explained why:

"In each dispensation, . . . the Lord has revealed anew the principles of the gospel. So that while the records of past dispensations, insofar as they are uncorrupted, testify to the truths of the gospel, still each dispensation has had revealed in its day sufficient truth to guide the people of the new dispensation, independent of the records of the past. . . . The gospel, as revealed to the Prophet Joseph Smith, is complete and is the word direct from heaven to this dispensation. It alone is sufficient to teach us the principles of eternal life."[14]

In frank and open terms, this means that though we love the Bible, we get our doctrine from modern revelation. As we read the Bible, we interpret it through what was revealed in the latter days—not the other way around. This important principle is a safeguard against doctrinal misdirection. We gladly use the words of the Bible to confirm, to bear witness to, and to illustrate the truths of modern revelation, but our knowledge of the gospel comes through what was revealed in the Restoration.

NOTES

1. For a discussion of the great and abominable church, see Kent P. Jackson, *From Apostasy to Restoration* (Salt Lake City: Deseret Book, 1996), 2–22.

2. Dean C. Jessee, ed., *Autobiographical and Historical Writings,* vol. 1 of *The Papers of Joseph Smith* series (Salt Lake City: Deseret Book, 1989–), 372.

3. Andrew F. Ehat and Lyndon W. Cook, eds., *The Words of Joseph Smith: The Contemporary Accounts of the Nauvoo Discourses of the Prophet Joseph* (Provo, Utah: Religious Studies Center, Brigham Young University, 1980), 211; spelling and capitalization standardized.

4. Ibid., 256.

5. Joseph Smith, *History of The Church of Jesus Christ of Latter-day Saints,* ed. B. H. Roberts, 2d ed. rev., 7 vols. (Salt Lake City: Deseret Book, 1957), 6:57.

6. In current English-language editions.

7. See Joseph Smith, *Joseph Smith's Commentary on the Bible,* comp. and ed. Kent P. Jackson (Salt Lake City: Deseret Book, 1994).

8. During the period in which he was engaged in his study of Hebrew, it was one of the most compelling and urgent interests in his life, as his journal attests. See Dean C. Jessee, ed., *Journal, 1832–1842,* vol. 2 of *Papers of Joseph Smith* series (Salt Lake City: Deseret Book, 1989–), 87–187.

9. See Ehat and Cook, eds., *Words of Joseph Smith.*

10. Ibid., 191.

11. Ibid., 345; punctuation and capitalization standardized.

12. Ezra Taft Benson, "Prepare Yourselves for the Great Day of the Lord," *Brigham Young University Fireside and Devotional Speeches, 1980–81* (Provo, Utah: Brigham Young University, 1981), 65.

13. Certainly the Doctrine and Covenants but also the Book of Mormon. See Mormon 8:34–35; Ezra Taft Benson, "The Book of Mormon—Keystone of Our Religion," *Ensign,* November 1986, 6–7.

14. Marion G. Romney, "A Glorious Promise," *Ensign,* January 1981, 2.

3

WHAT IS THE JOSEPH SMITH TRANSLATION?

S HORTLY AFTER THE CHURCH was organized, the Prophet Joseph Smith was instructed by the Lord to undertake a careful reading of the Bible to revise and make corrections in accordance with the inspiration he would receive. The result was a work of profound significance for the Church that included the revelation of many important truths and the restoration of many of the "precious things" that Nephi had foreseen would be taken from the Bible (1 Ne. 13:28–29; see also vv. 23–27). The inspired process began in June 1830. Over the next three years, the Prophet made changes, additions, and corrections as were given him by divine inspiration while he filled his calling to provide a more correct translation.[1] Collectively, these are called the Joseph Smith Translation (JST) or, as Joseph Smith referred to it, the New Translation. These titles are properly used for the text as written on the original manuscript pages. The title *Inspired Version* (I.V.) refers to the edited, printed version, published in book form in Independence, Missouri, by the Community of Christ (formerly the Reorganized Church of Jesus Christ of Latter Day Saints).[2]

HISTORY

The first revelation of the Joseph Smith Translation is what we now call Moses 1 in the Pearl of Great Price. The preface to the book of Genesis, it begins the earliest Old Testament manuscript of the New Translation, designated OT1.[3] Serving as scribes on OT1 were Oliver Cowdery, John Whitmer, Emma Smith, and Sidney Rigdon.[4] Dictating the text of the New Translation to these scribes, the Prophet had progressed to Genesis 24:41,[5] when he set aside Genesis to begin translating the New Testament as he was instructed by the Lord on 7 March 1831 (see D&C 45:60–62).

The earliest New Testament manuscript, designated NT1, includes most of the book of Matthew. It was begun at Matthew 1:1 on 8 March 1831 and ends at Matthew 26:71. The scribe was Sidney Rigdon. A second New Testament manuscript, NT2, begins with a copy of the first manuscript and then continues the dictated text through John 5. At that point, in February 1832, the Prophet ceased dictating the text in full to his scribes and developed an abbreviated notation system in which words to be corrected were marked in a Bible (crossed out, circled, or otherwise identified), and only the references and replacement words were recorded on the manuscript. John Whitmer was the copyist of Matthew 1:1–26:71, transcribing that material from NT1. Taking dictation from the Prophet for the rest of the New Testament were John Whitmer, Sidney Rigdon, Frederick G. Williams, and one other yet-unidentified scribe.[6]

The Bible that Joseph Smith used to assist in his translation was a King James Version purchased 8 October 1829 at the

E. B. Grandin bookstore in Palmyra, New York, where the Book of Mormon was being typeset at the time.[7] The text of the Prophet's Bible is very close to that of the 1769 King James Version used in the Church today, but the words in his Bible are modernized in some instances, and in hundreds of verses the punctuation is different.[8]

Following the completion of the New Testament on 2 February 1833, Joseph Smith returned to his work on the Old Testament.[9] A second Old Testament manuscript, designated OT2,[10] begins with a copy of the first manuscript (OT1). John Whitmer had made the copy two years earlier when Joseph Smith and Sidney Rigdon began working on the New Testament. The Prophet soon shifted to the abbreviated notation system for this manuscript also, marking passages in the Bible that needed to be changed and dictating the revisions to his scribes as they recorded them on the manuscript. Assisting him on OT2 were John Whitmer and Frederick G. Williams. Joseph Smith served as his own scribe for some sections.[11] At the end of the Old Testament manuscript, after the book of Malachi, the following words are written in large letters: "Finished on the 2d day of July 1833." That same day the Prophet wrote to Church members in Missouri and told them, "We this day finished the translating of the Scriptures for which we returned gratitude to our heavenly father."[12]

During the course of the Prophet's work with the Bible, changes were made in about thirteen hundred Old Testament verses and in about twenty-one hundred verses in the New Testament.[13] Most of the changes are rewordings of the existing King James translation text. But other changes involve the addition of new material—in some cases substantial amounts. Presumably every book in the Bible was examined, but no changes were made in thirteen of them.[14] The books with no

corrections are identified on the manuscripts with brief nota-
tions like "Micah—Correct."[15] Ecclesiastes is the only book not
mentioned at all. Regarding another book, the manuscript
notes: "The Songs of Solomon are not Inspired writings."[16]

On many pages of the manuscripts are revisions that were
made after the original dictation. Some are simply mechanical,
such as the insertion of punctuation, verse numbering,
or changes to upper or lower case. There are hundreds of
examples of each of these. But in many other cases, words were
added to the text or existing wording was revised. Many of
these changes simply correct errors in the original recording,
such as when the Prophet's eyes skipped words while he was
dictating or when his scribe recorded words incorrectly. But
some insertions revise the writing or add words or phrases to
produce new meanings not recorded in the original dictation.
Some of these insertions required more room than was available between the lines of the text and were written on small
pieces of paper and attached in place with straight pins—the
nineteenth-century equivalent of paper clips or staples.

Even though some of the later corrections provide important clarifications and insights, the overwhelming majority of
significant contributions of the Joseph Smith Translation were
made during the original dictation. We can identify almost all
of the handwriting of the original recording and thus know who
the Prophet's scribes were in most instances. Of the subsequent
changes in wording, most are in the hand of Sidney Rigdon.
Some were written by Frederick G. Williams and only a very
few by Joseph Smith. Sidney Rigdon served as a scribe for
Joseph Smith until the fall of 1833, and Frederick G. Williams
served until about December 1835.[17] The revisions inserted
after the original dictation were thus probably made before the
mid-1830s and most likely before, or not long after, Joseph

Smith pronounced the translation "finished" in July 1833. These facts cast doubt on the common belief that he continued to revise the wording of the translation through the rest of his life. From 2 July 1833 on, there are no references in his diaries and letters to his making additional changes. There are several statements regarding the preparation of the manuscript for publication, which probably refer not to changes in the translation but to the many insertions of punctuation, capitalization, and verse numbering. We cannot identify the handwritings or the dates for those small changes, but most were probably made by clerks working under the Prophet's direction.

Was the translation finished? In general, the answer is yes. The Bible, even in its purest and fullest form, never contained the complete records of those who are mentioned in it. The book of Genesis, for example, is a revelation to Moses that provides mere summaries of important lives and events. Certainly other truths could have been revealed to the Prophet to record in the New Translation and other additions could have been inserted to make it more complete, but from July 1833 onward, Joseph Smith spoke not of translating the Bible but of publishing it, which he intended to accomplish "as soon as possible."[18] He sought to find the means to print it as a book, and he repeatedly encouraged the Saints to donate money for it. But for a variety of reasons, including money and the other priorities of the Saints, it was not printed in his lifetime.[19] Because excerpts were published in the Church's newspapers and elsewhere, some sections were available for early Church members.[20] Still, when Joseph Smith was martyred in 1844, he had not seen the realization of his desire to have the entire New Translation appear in print.

In the decades after the Prophet's death, Latter-day Saints in Utah lacked access to the manuscripts of the New

Translation and had only limited knowledge of how it was produced. None of the participants in the translation process were with the Church when the Saints moved west in 1846.[21] These and related circumstances resulted in many misconceptions about the New Translation that eventually made their way into Latter-day Saint culture. Among those misconceptions are the beliefs that the Prophet did not finish the translation and that it was not intended to be published in his lifetime. Careful research by Robert J. Matthews shows that these ideas are refuted in Joseph Smith's own words.[22] But was the New Translation ready to go to press when Joseph Smith died? Brother Matthews has pointed out: "The basic conclusion seems to be that the *work* of translation was acceptable as far as the Lord required it of the Prophet at that time, but the *manuscript* was not fully prepared for the press."[23] Work still needed to be done to refine the verse divisions and to provide consistent spelling and punctuation, and some of the individual changes had resulted in unevenness in wording that had not yet been smoothed out. In short, although the inspired work of translating had been completed by Joseph Smith as far as was intended, the text was still in need of editing when he died.

TYPES OF CHANGES

The Lord called Joseph Smith "a seer, a revelator, a translator" (D&C 107:92), and in several Doctrine and Covenants passages the Lord endorsed the New Translation (see D&C 35:20; 43:12–13; 73:3–4; 90:13; 93:53; 94:10). Joseph Smith was appointed by God to do the work (see D&C 76:15), concerning which the Lord said, "And the scriptures shall be given, even as they are in mine own bosom, to the salvation of mine own elect" (D&C 35:20). Because God revealed the Joseph Smith

Translation for the salvation of his elect, Latter-day Saints embrace it and use it as they do the Book of Mormon, the Doctrine and Covenants, and the Pearl of Great Price. The Prophet called it a "translation," though it did not involve creating a new rendering from Hebrew or Greek manuscripts. He never claimed to have consulted any text for it other than his English Bible, but he "translated" it in the sense of conveying it in a new form.

It appears that several different kinds of changes were involved in the process, and though it is difficult to know with certainty the nature or origin of any particular change, the following five categories seem to include all the revisions in the New Translation.[24]

1. Restoration of original text. Because Nephi tells us that "many plain and precious things" would be "taken away" from the Bible (1 Ne. 13:28), we can be certain that the Joseph Smith Translation includes the restoration of content that was in original manuscripts. To Moses, the Lord foretold the removal of material from his record and its restoration in the latter days: "Thou shalt write the things which I shall speak. And in a day when the children of men shall esteem my words as naught and take many of them from the book which thou shalt write, behold, I will raise up another like unto thee; and they shall be had again among the children of men—among as many as shall believe" (Moses 1:40–41). Joseph Smith was the one whom the Lord raised up to restore the words of Moses, as well as lost material from the words of other Bible writers. But Joseph Smith did not restore the very words of lost texts, because they were in Hebrew or Greek (or other ancient languages), and the New Translation was to be in English. Thus his translation, in the English idiom of his own day, would restore the meaning and the message of original passages but not necessarily the literary trappings that accompanied them when they were first put to writing.

2. *Restoration of what was once said or done but which was never in the Bible.* Joseph Smith stated, "From what we can draw from the scriptures relative to the teachings of heaven we are induced to think, that much instruction has been given to man since the beginning which we have not."[25] Perhaps the Joseph Smith Translation includes teachings or events in the ministries of prophets, apostles, or Jesus himself that were never recorded anciently. It may include material of which the biblical writers were unaware, or which they chose not to include or neglected to record (cf. 3 Ne. 23:6–13).

3. *Editing to make the Bible more understandable for modern readers.* Many of the individual changes in the Joseph Smith Translation are in this category. There are numerous instances in which the Prophet rearranged word order to make a text read more easily or modernized its language. Examples of modernization of language include the many changes from *wot* to *know*,[26] from *an* to *a* before words that begin with *h*, from *saith* to *said*, from *that* and *which* to *who*, and from *ye* and *thee* to *you*.[27] In some instances Joseph Smith added short expansions to make the text less ambiguous. For example, in several places the word *he* is replaced by a personal name, thus making the meaning more clear, as in Genesis 14:20 (KJV "And he gave" = JST "And Abram gave") and in Genesis 18:32 (KJV "And he said, . . . And he said" = JST "And Abraham said . . . And the Lord said").

These examples are merely word choices and usually have no bearing on how the original text is to be interpreted. But other modernizations may have a more significant aim. Some could be called "cultural translations"—the conversion of aspects of ancient culture into modern counterparts to make them communicate better to modern readers. An example might include 1 Thessalonians 5:26, in which "Greet all the brethren with an holy *kiss*" is changed to "Greet all the brethren with a holy *salutation*" (see also Rom. 16:16; 1 Cor. 16:20; 2 Cor. 13:12). It is likely that the King James text here accurately represents Paul's original words and intent. Yet to modern Western readers, unaccustomed to Mediterranean displays of friendship and brotherhood, Paul's words might miscommunicate and misdirect, and thus the Prophet made a change.[28]

4. Editing to bring wording of a passage into harmony with truth found in other revelations or elsewhere in the Bible. Joseph Smith said, "[There are] many things in the Bible which do not, as they now stand, accord with the revelation of the Holy Ghost to me."[29] Where there were inaccuracies in the Bible, regardless of their source, it was well within the scope of the Prophet's calling to change what needed to be changed. Where modern revelation had given a clearer view of a doctrine preserved less adequately in the Bible, it was appropriate for Joseph Smith to add a correction, whether or not that correction reflects what was on the ancient original manuscript. And where a passage was inconsistent with information elsewhere in the Bible itself, a change needed to be made.

Three examples may illustrate this kind of change. First, the Gospel of John records the statement, "No man hath seen God at any time" (John 1:18), which contradicts the experience of Joseph Smith (JS–H 1:17–20) as well as biblical examples of prophets seeing God (e.g., Ex. 24:9–11; 33:11; Num. 12:6–8; Isa. 6:1; Amos 9:1). The Joseph Smith Translation change at John 1:19 clarifies the text. Second, the Gospel of Matthew contains what appears to be a misunderstanding of the donkey used in Jesus' triumphal entry (see Matt. 21:2–3, 7). The Joseph Smith Translation revises the text to agree with the clearer accounts in Mark, Luke, and John. Third, Matthew 27:3–5 and Acts 1:16–19 contain conflicting information about Judas' death. The Joseph Smith Translation revises Matthew to harmonize the two accounts.

5. *Changes to provide modern readers with teachings that were not written by original authors.* Perhaps there are changes in the Joseph Smith Translation in which Joseph Smith was inspired to alter or adapt an author's original words, or even to remove them from their original context, to reveal teachings needed by the latter-day Church. Elder Bruce R. McConkie, speaking of the differences between the early chapters of Genesis in the Bible and in the Joseph Smith Translation, said, "Both of them are true." He stated that John 1:1 in the Bible "is true," yet the Joseph Smith Translation gives it "an entirely new perspective." "These are illustrations of the fact that there can be two translations of the same thing and both of them can be true."[30] There is an important Joseph Smith Translation change at Romans 13 in which Paul's teaching regarding the Saints' submission to secular political power is changed to submission to the authorities of the Church. Perhaps both versions are correct. If the Bible preserves accurately Paul's original thoughts and intent, then the Joseph Smith Translation revision would be viewed as a latter-day revelation intended to instruct us on a topic not anticipated by Paul.[31]

Some have dismissed the Joseph Smith Translation because its changes are not verified in ancient manuscripts.[32] The claim is that if the Joseph Smith Translation revisions were justifiable, they would agree with the earliest existing manuscripts of the biblical books. But this reasoning is misdirected in two ways. First, it assumes that all changes in the Joseph Smith Translation are intended to restore original text, a claim made neither by the Joseph Smith Translation itself nor by the

Prophet Joseph Smith. Second, it assumes that extant ancient manuscripts accurately reproduce the original text. Joseph Smith taught that "many important points, touching the salvation of man, had been taken from the Bible, or lost before it was compiled,"[33] corroborating Nephi's testimony that "many plain and precious things" would be "taken away" from it (1 Ne. 13:28; see also vv. 23–27, 29). Unfortunately, the earliest fragments of most New Testament manuscripts date from a century or two after the originals were first written, and the earliest Old Testament manuscripts date from hundreds of years after the authors wrote their books. Given the prophetic assurance that changes would be made in the texts, and given the ample window of time during which those changes could have been made, we cannot have confidence that the earliest existing manuscripts today are identical to those that "came from the pen of the original writers."[34]

LATER HISTORY

In 1851 Elder Franklin D. Richards of the Quorum of the Twelve Apostles was serving as president of the British mission in Liverpool. Sensing a need to make available for the British Saints some of Joseph Smith's revelations that had been published already in America, he compiled a mission pamphlet entitled *The Pearl of Great Price*. In it he included, among other important texts, the excerpts from the Prophet's New Translation of the Bible that had been published already in Church periodicals and elsewhere: the first few chapters of Genesis and Matthew 24. Over the course of time, Elder Richards's compilation became a popular item of literature among members of the Church. Since most of the British Saints eventually emigrated to America, so also did the popularity of

The Pearl of Great Price. In the 1870s the decision was made to prepare it for churchwide distribution. The first Salt Lake edition was published in 1878. In the October 1880 general conference it was presented to the assembled membership for a vote sustaining it as canonized scripture, and it was accepted as binding on the Church.[35] Since then, the Pearl of Great Price has been one of the standard works of the Church, and the few chapters of the Joseph Smith Translation in it have been recognized not only as divine revelation—which they always were—but also as integral parts of our scripture and doctrine.

When Joseph Smith died, the manuscripts of the New Translation were in the possession not of the Church but of his family, who remained in Illinois when the leaders of the Church and the majority of the Saints moved to the West. In 1867 the Reorganized Church of Jesus Christ of Latter Day Saints (now Community of Christ) published the New Translation under the title *The Holy Scriptures, Translated and Corrected by the Spirit of Revelation. By Joseph Smith, Jr., the Seer.* It has been known popularly by the name *Inspired Version* since the nineteenth century. That name was added officially in an edition of 1936, but it is appropriate to refer to it as such since its first publication. As mentioned, at the time of Joseph Smith's death, the punctuation and verse numbering on the manuscripts were still in need of refinement. The punctuation and versification of the printed *Inspired Version* generally do not follow what is written on the Joseph Smith Translation manuscripts but were supplied by the 1866–67 RLDS publication committee. It appears that they modeled their work after the King James translation rather than following what was on the manuscripts.

Because the Saints in Utah knew little about the New Translation and did not have access to its original documents, it was not widely used within our Church, aside from the excerpts that are part of the Pearl of Great Price. Over the years lack of knowledge about the New Translation led some Latter-day Saints not only to misunderstand it and the process by which it was created but to question the accuracy of the printed *Inspired Version*. Some Latter-day Saints came to view the New Translation with reservations.[36] During the 1960s and 1970s, Robert Matthews conducted exhaustive research on the manuscripts and on Joseph Smith's marked Bible.[37] His study confirmed the general integrity of the printed *Inspired Version* and taught us many things about the New Translation and how it was produced. In the process Professor Matthews brought the Joseph Smith Translation to the attention of members of the Church.[38]

In 1979, when the Church published a Latter-day Saint edition of the Bible in the English language, generous amounts of material from the New Translation were included in footnotes and in an appendix.[39] In subsequent years excerpts from the Joseph Smith Translation were included in the "Guide to the Scriptures," a combination concordance–Bible dictionary published with the LDS scriptures in languages other than English. To these are added a volume published by the Religious Studies Center at Brigham Young University, which includes a facsimile transcription of all the original Joseph Smith Translation manuscripts.[40] A significant aspect of these publications is that they have made the Joseph Smith Translation accessible to an extent that it never has been before. Now general authorities, curriculum writers, scholars, and students can draw freely from it in their research and writing, bringing the Joseph Smith Translation to its rightful place alongside the other great revelations of the Prophet Joseph Smith. It is, as Elder Dallin H. Oaks observed, "a member of the royal family of scripture" that "should be noticed and honored on any occasion when it is present."[41]

NOTES

1. The most extensive treatment of the Joseph Smith Translation is Robert J. Matthews, *"A Plainer Translation": Joseph Smith's Translation of the Bible—A History and Commentary* (Provo, Utah: Brigham Young University Press, 1975). The research of Robert J. Matthews is the foundation on which subsequent research on the Joseph Smith Translation has been built. I thankfully acknowledge his contributions to what I know about this subject, through his writings and countless personal conversations.

2. First published in 1867, the most recent edition was published in 1991. References to the *Inspired Version (I.V.)* hereafter are to the chapter and verse numbers in the printed *Inspired Version,* which differ sometimes from the traditional biblical references and from those written on the Joseph Smith Translation manuscripts.

3. All of the Joseph Smith Translation manuscripts are located in the archives of the Community of Christ in Independence, Missouri. In many earlier publications, an old archival numbering system is used for the manuscripts, resulting from an early misunderstanding of the order in which the manuscripts were written. OT1 was previously designated OT2.

4. Oliver Cowdery (Gen. 1:1–4:18; *I.V.* Gen. 1:1–5:28; Moses 1:1–5:43); John Whitmer (Gen. 4:18–5:11; *I.V.* Gen. 5:29–6:16; 6:53–7:1; Moses 5:43–6:18; 6:52–7:1); Emma Smith (Gen. 5:12–21; *I.V.* Gen. 6:17–53; Moses 6:19–52); Sidney Rigdon (Gen. 5:22–24:41; *I.V.* Gen. 7:2–24:42; Moses 7:2–8:30).

5. *I.V.* Genesis 24:42.

6. John Whitmer (Matt. 26:1–Mark 9:1); Sidney Rigdon (Mark 9:2–2 Thess. 2:3; 2 Thess. 3:1–Heb. 5:8; Heb. 6:9–7:26; 8:4–9:26; 10:1–21; 11:12–13:5; James 2:1–2 Pet. 3:18; 1 John 3:9–Jude; Rev. 1:20–11:4); Frederick G. Williams (Rev. 12:1–22:9); unidentified scribe (2 Thess. 2:7–9; Heb. 6:1–8; 7:27; 9:28; 11:1; James 1; 1 John 1:1–3:8; Rev. 1:1–16).

7. On the first sheet of the Bible inside the front cover is this inscription in Oliver Cowdery's handwriting: "The Book of the Jews And the Property of / Joseph Smith Junior and Oliver Cowdery / Bought October the 8th 1829, at Egbert B Grandins / Book Store Palmyra Wayne County New York. / Price $3.75 / H[o]liness to the L[ord]."

8. See Kent P. Jackson, "Joseph Smith's Cooperstown Bible: The Bible Used in the Joseph Smith Translation in its Historical Context," *BYU Studies* 40, no. 1 (2001): 41–70. The Bible used by the Prophet was published in 1828 by the H. and E. Phinney Company of Cooperstown, New York. It is housed in the Community of Christ Archives in Independence, Missouri. Because this was the Bible that Joseph Smith used in the New Translation, it (and not the current KJV revision) is the default text that underlies the Joseph Smith Translation. Aside from the many punctuation differences, the most common difference is that the Prophet's Bible uses *a* before words that begin with a pronounced letter *h,* as in "*a* house" (1 Kgs. 5:3) and "*a* hundred" (Gen. 11:25), whereas the King James revision used in the LDS edition of the Bible (1979) uses the archaic *an:* "*an* house" and "*an* hundred."

9. Under the date of 2 February 1833, the Prophet's minute book records: "This day completed the translation and the reviewing of the New Testament." Kirtland High Council Minute Book, 2 February 1833, 8, Archives, The Church of Jesus Christ of Latter-day Saints, Salt Lake City.

10. Formerly OT3.

11. John Whitmer (copy of Gen. 1:1–24:41 [*I.V.* Gen. 24:42]; Moses 1–8); Frederick G. Williams (scribe for Gen. 24:41 [*I.V.* Gen. 24:42]–Neh. 10:30; Ps. 11–15; Ps. 17–Mal.); Joseph Smith (Neh. 11–Ps. 10 and Ps. 16).

12. Joseph Smith, Sidney Rigdon, and Frederick G. Williams to the Brethren in Zion, 2 July 1833, Joseph Smith Letter Book 1, 51 (Ms. 155, Box 2, folder 1), Joseph Smith Collection, Archives, The Church of Jesus Christ of Latter-day Saints, Salt Lake City.

13. Matthews, *"A Plainer Translation,"* 425.

14. Esther, Ecclesiastes, Song of Solomon, Lamentations, Obadiah, Micah, Nahum, Habakkuk, Zephaniah, Haggai, Malachi, 2 John, and 3 John.

15. OT2, page 118.

16. OT2, page 97.

17. Williams stated that he began on 20 July 1832 and served as scribe for three years and four months. See Frederick G. Williams, "Frederick Granger Williams of the First Presidency of the Church," *BYU Studies* 12, no. 3 (spring 1972): 250, n. 21.

18. "You will see by these revelations that we have to print the new translation here at kirtland for which we will prepare as soon as possible." Joseph Smith, Sidney Rigdon, and Frederick G. Williams to Edward Partridge, 6 August 1833, Letters Sent, Oversized (Ms. 155, Box 6, folder 2), Joseph Smith Collection, Archives, The Church of Jesus Christ of Latter-day Saints, Salt Lake City.

19. The evidence is collected in Robert J. Matthews, "Joseph Smith's Efforts to Publish His Bible Translation," *Ensign,* January 1983, 57–64.

20. *The Evening and the Morning Star* 1, no. 3 (August 1832): 2–3 (Moses 7); 1, no. 10 (March 1833): 1 (Moses 6:43–68); 1, no. 11 (April 1833): 1 (Moses 5:1–16); 1, no. 11 (April 1833): 1–2 (Moses 8:13–30); *Doctrine and Covenants of the Church of the Latter Day Saints* (Kirtland, Ohio: F. G. Williams and Co., 1835), "Lecture First," 5 (Heb. 11:1); "Lecture Second," 13–18 (Moses 2:26–29; 3:15–17, 19–20; 4:14–19, 22–25; 5:1, 4–9, 19–23, 32–40); *Times and Seasons* 4, no. 5 (16 January 1843): 71–73 (Moses 1); Peter Crawley, *A Descriptive Bibliography of the Mormon Church, Volume One 1830–1847* (Provo, Utah: Religious Studies Center, Brigham Young University, 1997), 60–61 (Matthew 24).

21. Joseph Smith (died 1844), Oliver Cowdery (excommunicated 1838; died in the Church 1848), John Whitmer (excommunicated 1838), Emma Smith (did not go west), Sidney Rigdon (excommunicated 1844), and Frederick G. Williams (excommunicated 1839; died in the Church 1842).

22. See Matthews, "Joseph Smith's Efforts."

23. Ibid., 64.

24. Categories somewhat similar to mine are found in Matthews, "A Plainer Translation," 253, and in Robert L. Millet, "Joseph Smith's Translation of the Bible: A Historical Overview," in *The Joseph Smith Translation: The Restoration of Plain and Precious Things,* ed. Monte S. Nyman and Robert L. Millet (Provo, Utah: Religious Studies Center, Brigham Young University, 1985), 43–45.

25. *The Evening and the Morning Star* 2, no. 18 (March 1834): 143.

26. The manuscript at Exodus 32:1 revises *wot* to *know* with a note that *know* "should be in the place of 'wot' in all places."

27. These changes are not universally consistent in the manuscripts.

28. Perhaps the changes at Genesis 24:2, 9 fit this same category.

29. Andrew F. Ehat and Lyndon W. Cook, eds., *The Words of Joseph Smith: The Contemporary Accounts of the Nauvoo Discourses of the Prophet Joseph* (Provo, Utah: Religious Studies Center, Brigham Young University, 1980), 211; spelling and capitalization standardized.

30. Mark L. McConkie, ed., *Doctrines of the Restoration: Sermons and Writings of Bruce R. McConkie* (Salt Lake City: Bookcraft, 1989), 269.

31. The footnotes in the LDS edition of the Bible to Romans 13:1 acknowledge both readings by including the Joseph Smith Translation changes as well as cross-references to "Citizenship," "Governments," and Doctrine and Covenants 58:21–22, which enjoins obedience to secular political authority.

32. E.g., Kevin L. Barney, "The Joseph Smith Translation and Ancient Texts of the Bible," *Dialogue: A Journal of Mormon Thought* 19, no. 3 (fall 1986): 85–102; Edward H. Ashment, "Making the Scriptures 'Indeed One in Our Hands,'" in *The Word of God: Essays on Mormon Scripture,* ed. Dan Vogel (Salt Lake City: Signature Book, 1990), 240–44, 252–53.

33. Dean C. Jessee, ed., *Autobiographical and Historical Writings,* vol. 1 of *The Papers of Joseph Smith* series (Salt Lake City: Deseret Book, 1989–), 372.

34. Ehat and Cook, eds., *Words of Joseph Smith,* 256.

35. The text of the book of Moses in the 1851 Pearl of Great Price was based on OT1. In the 1878 edition, the Moses text was taken from the 1867 RLDS *Inspired Version.*

36. See Dallin H. Oaks, "Scripture Reading, Revelation, and Joseph Smith's Translation of the Bible," in *Plain and Precious Truths Restored: The Doctrinal and Historical Significance of the Joseph Smith Translation,* ed. Robert L. Millet and Robert J. Matthews (Salt Lake City: Bookcraft, 1995), 5–15.

37. Robert J. Matthews, "A Study of the Doctrinal Significance of Certain Textual Changes Made by the Prophet Joseph Smith in the Four Gospels of the Inspired Version of the New Testament" (M.A. thesis, Brigham Young University, 1960), and "A Study of the Text of the Inspired Revision of the Bible" (Ph.D. dissertation, Brigham Young

University, 1968). "*A Plainer Translation*" was published in 1975. See Millet, "Historical Overview," 38–41.

38. See Thomas E. Sherry, "Changing Attitudes toward Joseph Smith's Translation of the Bible," in *Plain and Precious Truths Restored,* ed. Millet and Matthews, 187–226.

39. The Joseph Smith Translation text was drawn from a November 1965 printing of the 1944 "Corrected Edition" of the *Inspired Version;* Matthews, personal communication. Matthews served on the committee that prepared the footnotes for the 1979 Bible publication.

40. Scott R. Faulring, Kent P. Jackson, and Robert J. Matthews, eds., *Joseph Smith's New Translation of the Bible: Original Manuscripts* (Provo, Utah: Religious Studies Center, Brigham Young University, 2002).

41. Oaks, "Scripture Reading," 13.

4

WHAT IS THE
OLD TESTAMENT?

THE WORD *TESTAMENT* MEANS COVENANT, and the Old Testament, which includes the covenant that God established with Israel at Sinai, obtains its name from that source. The New Testament derives its name from the new covenant of Christianity, which is contained within its pages. Key scriptural passages upon which this terminology is in part based are Jeremiah 31:31–33, along with New Testament references to Jeremiah's words (e.g., Heb. 8:8–13), and Jesus' words at the Last Supper (see Matt. 26:28; Mark 14:24; Luke 22:20; 1 Cor. 11:25). Jeremiah spoke of a new covenant that God would establish with his people, not like the old covenant written on tablets of stone but a new covenant to be written in human hearts. Jesus introduced the sacrament as a "new testament" (Matt. 26:28). Though the terms *Old Testament* and *New Testament* may not be entirely appropriate as titles for the two records—either historically or doctrinally—still, the names convey well the idea of the covenant of Sinai being the precursor and forerunner to the greater covenant of the gospel. And certainly the sacred record that we call the Old Testament serves well to set the stage and prepare the way for the greater revelation to come.

It is difficult to define what the Old Testament is; a more productive quest is to define what the Old Testament contains. The Old Testament is a collection of books, consisting of thirty-nine books that record God's dealings with his covenant people of the era of Moses—ancient Israel. The core of its record extends from the call of Moses, ca. 1250 B.C., to the time of Nehemiah, ca. 432 B.C. Yet it also includes a record that extends as far into the past as the Creation and prophecies that extend as far into the future as the glorification of the earth. Its scope, therefore, is limitless, even as the scope of the Lord's work is limitless.

In the present form and organization of modern Bible translations, the sacred record of ancient Israel can be divided into four sections: the prologue, the historical core, the Writings, and the Prophets.

THE PROLOGUE

The prologue to the Old Testament is the book of Genesis. It may be called a prologue because it is a retrospection—a flashback—from the basic historical narrative that is the core of the Old Testament. Genesis provides the essential backdrop to that narrative, which begins with the work of Moses. Indeed, modern revelation teaches us that the Old Testament begins with Moses (see Moses 1:40; 2:1; and the discussion in chapter 5 of this volume).

Genesis is significant not only for the account of the Creation but also for the material that follows. In it we learn of humankind's temporary sojourn in Eden and expulsion into mortality. We trace the parallel developments of the work of God and the work of Satan among men, and we follow the line

The Books of the Old Testament

THE PROLOGUE	HISTORICAL CORE	THE WRITINGS	THE PROPHETS
Genesis	Exodus	Esther	*Major Prophets*
	Leviticus	Job	Isaiah
	Numbers	Psalms	Jeremiah
	Deuteronomy	Proverbs	Ezekiel
	Joshua	Ecclesiastes	Daniel
	Judges	Song of Solomon	
	Ruth	Lamentations	*Minor Prophets*
	1–2 Samuel		Hosea
	1–2 Kings		Joel
	1–2 Chronicles		Amos
	Ezra		Obadiah
	Nehemiah		Jonah
			Micah
			Nahum
			Habakkuk
			Zephaniah
			Haggai
			Zechariah
			Malachi

These categories are based on content rather than on date, authorship, or origin. According to Nephi (see 1 Ne. 5:11–13), Laban's plates of brass contained the "five books of Moses" (which included a record of the Creation and Adam and Eve), a record of the Jews from the beginning to the days of Lehi, and the words of the prophets from "the beginning" to Jeremiah's time. Nephi's emphasis was clearly on what the Jews later called "the Law" and "the Prophets," that is, the Pentateuch, the historical books, and the Prophets. It is not known whether any of the Writings were included on the plates of brass. Some of the literary material in the Old Testament was compiled after Lehi's time.

of patriarchal priesthood from Adam to Joseph. But the emphasis in the first book of the Bible is clearly on the patriarchs and their children. Only eleven chapters touch on all the history from the Creation to Abraham. The remaining thirty-nine chapters deal with the lives and family relationships of three men—Abraham, Isaac, and Jacob. Genesis was written for their descendants, from the time of Moses and later, with messages ideally suited for their needs.

THE HISTORICAL CORE

The core of the Old Testament is the large body of historical material that extends from the calling of Moses through the career of Nehemiah (ca. 1250–432 B.C.).[1] This core includes Exodus, Leviticus, Numbers, Deuteronomy, Joshua, Judges, Ruth, 1–2 Samuel, 1–2 Kings, 1–2 Chronicles, Ezra, and Nehemiah. Written by a variety of authors, these books chronicle the history of Israel from its reconstruction in the days of Moses to the end of the Old Testament period. They constitute the historical framework to which are added the Genesis prologue and the collections of Writings and the Prophets.

Like the Book of Mormon, the Old Testament teaches its messages in large part through history. In its pages we can see how God is active in the affairs of humankind and how men and women have responded, or failed to respond, to the efforts of God and his chosen servants to bless their lives. Judging from some inconsistencies and historical problems in the record, it seems that the anonymous historians of the Old Testament were not all equally inspired and perhaps did not all enjoy the same quality of source materials.[2] But these noble, pious historians wrote from a perspective of deep personal commitment and obedience to the Lord's will. Their objective in writing is obvious: they hoped that future generations would learn through the examples of the past not to make the mistakes that had been made before and to duplicate the behavior of those who had lived righteously. Sadly, most of the lessons modern readers can learn from the Old Testament are from bad examples.[3]

The historical books of the Old Testament, including Genesis, make up the largest group in the Bible: 668 pages (in the LDS edition of the Bible in English), or 56.4 percent of the 1184-page Old Testament. In comparison, there are 404 pages in the New Testament and 531 pages in the Book of Mormon (the 1981 edition in English). Certainly there is much to learn about life from the events recorded in the Old Testament. As Paul wrote, "Now all these things happened unto them for ensamples: and they are written for our admonition, upon whom the ends of the world are come" (1 Cor. 10:11).[4]

THE WRITINGS

Translations in modern languages unfortunately place the literary works of the Old Testament, called the Writings, in a group before the books of the prophets, suggesting a priority either in date or value. The ancient grouping places them last.[5] The Writings include the following books: Esther, Job, Psalms, Proverbs, Ecclesiastes, the Song of Solomon (also known as the Song of Songs), and Lamentations (which appears in modern translations between Jeremiah and Ezekiel). Several of these books belong to a category of writing called wisdom literature, in which wisdom, or the capacity to go through life prudently and successfully, is conveyed through various literary styles. Perhaps the finest example of wisdom literature is the book of Proverbs, a collection of brief sayings that convey wisdom from one generation to the next. The book of Psalms, the hymnbook of ancient Israel, is considered by many to be unparalleled in its expression of Israelite devotion.

It seems safe to say that not all parts of the Writings are of equal inspiration. We do not know much about authorship or date of composition of some of the material. Joseph Smith stated, "The Songs of Solomon are not Inspired writings."[6] In addition, some Latter-day Saints find limited spiritual fulfillment in Ecclesiastes, which has a pessimism that seems to contradict the general mood of the Bible, or in Esther, which does not even mention God. And some of the Proverbs seem to focus on worldly values rather than on spiritual things. Although these books may not compare well in every way with the divine pronouncements in Genesis or in the prophetic books, they are nevertheless useful and instructive, and important lessons of life may be gleaned from them.

The Writings include 200 pages of the Old Testament, or 16.9 percent of the total number of pages in that volume of scripture.

THE PROPHETS

The last division in modern Bible translations contains the words of the prophets. Unlike most of the other books of the Bible, which are anonymous, the prophetic books are identified by the name of the author (except in the case of Jonah, an anonymous work named for the prophet in the story). These are commonly divided into two groups: the Major Prophets, which are Isaiah, Jeremiah, Ezekiel, and Daniel; and the Minor Prophets, which are Hosea, Joel, Amos, Obadiah, Jonah, Micah, Nahum, Habakkuk, Zephaniah, Haggai, Zechariah, and Malachi. The division between "major" and "minor" is based solely on the length of the books and not on the importance or quality of the content.

The Bible treats its prophetic material differently from the way the Book of Mormon does. In the Nephite record the words of the prophets are integrated into the historical account. For example, in the book of Alma, Mormon includes historical narrative as well as letters and transcripts (or summaries) of sermons and prophecies. In the Old Testament the prophetic content is found in a separate collection, and the prophetic books seem to have been compiled for the most part independently of the historical framework.[7]

The Prophets comprise 317 pages, or 26.8 percent, of the Old Testament.

READING AND UNDERSTANDING THE OLD TESTAMENT

Many Latter-day Saint readers find the Old Testament to be the most difficult part of the standard works of the Church. Yet rather than pay the necessary price to discover its beautiful truths, they avoid it. Admittedly, the Old Testament presents special challenges that require special solutions, but those solutions are within the reach of most of us, and the rewards for our efforts will be substantial.

Travelers outside their homelands often experience perplexing cultural and language barriers. Because the Old Testament is the product of a culture vastly different from our own, and because it was written in languages that relatively few members of the Church can read, barriers stand in the way for most of us. Even in translation, the Bible presents challenges. For example, in English-speaking countries, the Church uses the King James Version, a translation that is centuries old and in a dialect that few modern readers can understand sufficiently without effort.[8] Using *any* translation, we depend on the skill and integrity of the translators. Yet despite these obstacles, students of the Bible who pay the price of diligent, prayerful study and thought will find great satisfaction in their reading. Hard work and patience are often required.

Principles taught in modern revelation suggest four keys to gaining the most from reading the Old Testament:

1. *Study the Old Testament in light of gospel truth that has been revealed in modern times.* Because of the Book of Mormon, the Doctrine and Covenants, the Pearl of Great Price, and the Joseph Smith Translation of the Bible, we have better access to the gospel of Christ than do others not blessed with modern revelation. Joseph Smith, a great student and teacher of the Bible, provided many invaluable explanations of biblical passages,[9] and the words of his prophetic successors have provided additional insights. Through the light of modern revelation we have a better view of the meaning of scripture. And with the perspective of the entire gospel plan, made known through the Restoration, we can understand God's dealings with men and women of the past in a way not possible otherwise. Nephi said that the modern scriptures "shall establish the truth" of the Bible "and shall make known the plain and precious things which have been taken away" from it. They will also "make known to all kindreds, tongues, and people, that the Lamb of God is the Son of the Eternal Father, and the Savior of the world; and that all men must come unto him, or they cannot be saved" (1 Ne. 13:40). Through an inspired latter-day addition to Genesis, we learn that the Bible and the Book of Mormon would "grow together unto the confounding of false doctrines, and laying down of contentions," and bring the Lord's people "to the knowledge of their fathers . . . and also to the knowledge of my covenants, saith the Lord."[10]

2. *Have the Holy Ghost.* Prayerful study of sacred scripture draws us close to the ultimate source of all knowledge. As Nephi taught, the companionship of the Spirit is indispensable

for scripture study (see 2 Ne. 25:4). But that companionship is available only to those whose lives are in harmony with God's will.

3. *Learn how the ancient writers expressed themselves.* Nephi observed his people's disadvantage with the writings of Isaiah because they did not know "the manner of prophesying among the Jews" (2 Ne. 25:1). Learning the Jews' "manner of prophesying" probably includes becoming familiar with the Bible's language, idioms, teaching methods, poetic styles, and literary techniques. Almost all of the material in the Writings and the Prophets is written in poetry. Because people in the ancient Near East (and elsewhere) viewed poetic writing as an exalted level of communication, in many cultures, including ancient Israel, the divine words were written in poetic verse.

The most common building block of Israelite poetry is parallelism. In a typical poetic verse, a concept is expressed twice (or more) in parallel phrases. The phrases most often mean approximately the same thing, but different words are chosen for each.[11] For example, in Deuteronomy 32:1–2, Moses said:

> Give ear, O ye heavens, and I will speak;
> and hear, O earth, the words of my mouth.

Notice the parallels in "give ear" and "hear," "heavens" and "earth," and "I will speak" and "the words of my mouth."

> My doctrine shall drop as the rain,
> my speech shall distil as the dew,
> as the small rain upon the tender herb,
> and as the showers upon the grass.

The "manner of prophesying" among the ancient Israelites also includes the frequent use of metaphor, a literary device in which a word or phrase meaning one thing is used to represent something else, suggesting a likeness between them. Familiar examples are "Judah is a lion's whelp" (Gen. 49:9) and "The Lord is my shepherd" (Ps. 23:1).

An allegory is a metaphor in story form, as in the examples of Zenos's narration of the olive tree (see Jacob 5) and Jesus' parables. Metaphor communicates well within its own cultural framework. It is artistic language, but it is intended to be understood. It suggests a likeness but usually not an equation, and frequently it is intended to bring forth only general feelings. Rarely are details important or intended to be dissected.

4. *Understand the Old Testament within the context in which it originated.* A knowledge of historical and cultural circumstances and the contemporary issues to which the Old Testament writers addressed themselves helps us to more fully understand what they wrote. Latter-day Saints recognize that it is impossible to understand the Doctrine and Covenants fully without a knowledge of contemporary events in Church history. Nephi, Mormon, and Moroni wove prophetic material into their historical narratives so we would know the context of the revelations recorded in the Book of Mormon. Much of the material in the Old Testament is based in cultural realities and historical circumstances that are foreign to us. Nephi, a native of the ancient Near East, stated that like other Jews he could understand Isaiah because he had lived in Jerusalem and knew "concerning the regions round about" (2 Ne. 25:6; see also v. 5). Just as with the Doctrine and Covenants, our study of the Old Testament should include an introduction into the world in which it originated and consultation of sources that explain the circumstances that led to events and revelations.[12]

As with anything else of value, there is a price to be paid to learn what there is to learn in the Old Testament. And as Joseph

Smith said concerning the Bible in general, "He who reads it oftenest will like it best."[13]

NOTES

1. The last datable historical event in the Old Testament is Nehemiah's second mission to Jerusalem, which took place in 432 B.C. (Neh. 13:6–7).

2. It is likely that the biblical historians would concur with the feelings of the Book of Mormon writer Moroni regarding imperfections in their work. See Book of Mormon Title Page and Ether 12:23–25.

3. Perhaps the finest example of interpreting and teaching from biblical history is found in 2 Kings 17:7–23, which is the discussion that follows the account of the fall of Samaria and the deportation of Israel.

4. An important discussion of historical writing in the Old Testament is David Noel Freedman, "Canon of the OT," in *The Interpreter's Dictionary of the Bible,* ed. G. A. Buttrick et al. (Nashville: Abingdon, 1962–76), supplementary vol., 130–36.

5. By Jesus' day the Jews saw the Old Testament as a three-fold collection: the Law, the Prophets, and the Writings.

6. Joseph Smith Translation manuscript OT2, page 97.

7. Exceptions include the Elijah and Elisha narratives in 1–2 Kings, the duplication of 2 Kings 18–20 in Isaiah 36–39, and the historical content of the book of Jeremiah.

8. The King James Version was published in 1611, but even then its language was often archaic, because the translators sought to retain as much as possible of the language of earlier English translations. The King James text used in the 1979 LDS edition of the Bible is a revision of 1769. It differs from the 1611 edition primarily in spelling and punctuation.

9. See Joseph Smith, *Joseph Smith's Commentary on the Bible,* comp. and ed. Kent P. Jackson (Salt Lake City: Deseret Book, 1994).

10. I.V. Genesis 50:31; 2 Nephi 3:12.

11. See Robert Alter, *The Art of Biblical Poetry* (New York: Basic Books, 1985).

12. The maps (both the 1979 and 2000 editions) and Bible

Dictionary in the LDS publication of the Bible are important resources. Attempts at helpful commentary by Latter-day Saint scholars are found in Kent P. Jackson and Robert L. Millet, ed., *Genesis to 2 Samuel*, vol. 3 of the *Studies in Scripture* series (Salt Lake City: Deseret Book, 1989); and Kent P. Jackson, ed., *1 Kings to Malachi*, vol. 4 of the *Studies in Scripture* series (Salt Lake City: Deseret Book, 1993), among others. Two responsible one-volume commentaries by Bible-believing non-Latter-day Saints are W. S. LaSor, D. A. Hubbard, and F. W. Bush, *Old Testament Survey* (Grand Rapids, Mich.: Eerdmans, 1982); and A. E. Hill and J. H. Walton, *A Survey of the Old Testament* (Grand Rapids, Mich.: Zondervan, 1991). Two major biblical encyclopedias are G. A. Buttrick et al., eds., *The Interpreter's Dictionary of the Bible*, 5 vols. (Nashville: Abingdon, 1962–76); and David Noel Freedman, ed., *The Anchor Bible Dictionary*, 6 vols. (Garden City, N.Y.: Doubleday, 1992). A standard volume that takes the history in the Old Testament seriously is John Bright, *A History of Israel*, 3d ed. (Philadelphia: Westminster, 1981).

13. Joseph Smith, *Teachings of the Prophet Joseph Smith*, sel. Joseph Fielding Smith (Salt Lake City: Deseret Book, 1976), 56.

5

WHO WROTE GENESIS?

THE OLD TESTAMENT DOES NOT TELL us that Moses wrote
the Pentateuch, the first five books of the Bible. But from
New Testament times to recent centuries, it has been understood commonly that Moses was the author of those books,
including the book of Genesis. An examination of the evidence
both in the Bible and in latter-day scripture and history brings
into focus both the question of authorship and its answer. I
believe, based on modern revelation and on the content of the
book itself, that Genesis does indeed come from Moses. His
time period provides the best setting for what the book contains, and Moses himself is the best candidate for having been
its author.[1]

EVIDENCE FROM THE BIBLE

The Bible preserves a few accounts of Moses' recording
God's words or keeping a record of his people. After a battle
with the Amalekites, the Lord commanded Moses to write the
account of Israel's miraculous victory "for a memorial in a

book" (Ex. 17:14). After God revealed his law, "Moses wrote all
the words of the Lord" (Ex. 24:4). God told Moses to write the
words that were revealed to him (see Ex. 34:27), so Moses
"wrote upon the tables the words of the covenant, the ten commandments" (Ex. 34:28). When the Israelites traveled in the
wilderness, "Moses wrote their goings out according to their
journeys by the commandment of the Lord" (Num. 33:2). And
after charging Joshua with leading Israel, "Moses wrote this law,
and delivered it unto the priests the sons of Levi," so it could
be read periodically before all the people (Deut. 31:9; see also
vv. 10–11, 24).

Unfortunately, these examples refer not to material in
Genesis but to material in Exodus, Leviticus, Numbers, and
Deuteronomy. These examples pertain to the revelations and
experiences of Moses' own lifetime, the very things that other
prophets recorded from their own days. Moreover, these passages do not tell us that Moses wrote the books, only that
Moses wrote information now contained in them.

Genesis is different from the books that chronicle the
history of Moses, because Genesis deals with events that took
place centuries before Moses' day. It contains passages that suggest parts of it came from sources that existed before the book
of Genesis was compiled. For example, Genesis 5 begins, "This
is the book" (see also Moses 6:8), and Genesis 2:4 in the
Septuagint, the ancient Greek translation of the Old Testament,
begins the same way. Chapters 10 and 36 contain lists that
seem to have been composed as separate documents from other
sources. A parallel is found in the book of Abraham, in which
Abraham tells us that he possessed "the records of the fathers"
that included information about the priesthood, the Creation,
and other things. He promised to "endeavor to write some of

these things." Perhaps his account of the Creation was taken from those earlier "records of the fathers" (Abr. 1:31).

Later Old Testament books credit the written law to Moses but make no mention of the authorship of Genesis (e.g., Josh. 8:31–32; Neh. 8:1).[2] The New Testament does the same (e.g., Luke 24:44; John 5:46–47).[3] Although Jewish and Christian traditions have attributed the authorship of Genesis to Moses, the Bible itself is silent on the matter. If Moses did write Genesis, we need to find it out from other sources.

EVIDENCE FROM THE JOSEPH SMITH TRANSLATION AND THE BOOK OF MORMON

The clearest evidence in scripture that Genesis material originated with Moses is found in the Joseph Smith Translation of the Bible. Moses, sometime after the call to his prophetic mission, saw in vision the endless works of the Father. Moses was told, "I will speak unto thee concerning this earth upon which thou standest; and thou shalt write the things which I shall speak" (Moses 1:40). Continuing, the Lord said: "I reveal unto you concerning this heaven, and this earth; write the words which I speak. . . . In the beginning I created the heaven, and the earth upon which thou standest" (Moses 2:1). With this begins the familiar Creation account of Genesis—a revealed flashback from the time of Moses. The Joseph Smith Translation also shows that the account of Adam and Eve in the Garden of Eden comes from Moses (Moses 4:1, 32). At the very least, we can say that the Creation and Eden accounts in Genesis (Gen. 1–3) are the writings of Moses, being revelations that he recorded as he was instructed. It seems likely that parts or all of the rest of the book came in a similar way.

The Book of Mormon prophet Nephi gives us other

information that suggests a Mosaic origin for the Bible's first books. The plates of brass, as Nephi stated, included "the five books of Moses." Those books "gave an account of the creation of the world, and also of Adam and Eve, who were our first parents" (1 Ne. 5:11; cf. 19:23). Nephi's description of their content ("an account of the creation of the world, and also of Adam and Eve") is far from comprehensive, but their content may correspond with that of Genesis, Exodus, Leviticus, Numbers, and Deuteronomy.[4] Even if Moses did not actually write the books, it is significant that they apparently were named after him on the plates of brass.

Examples from Scripture and History

A brief look at how the Book of Mormon was compiled may assist us to understand the composition of Genesis and other parts of the Bible. The Book of Mormon provides clear examples of prophets as record keepers and shows that the writing of sacred history is frequently an aspect of the prophetic calling (e.g., 1 Ne. 9:3–5; Alma 37:1–2). The book as we have it, however, is not the work of Benjamin, Alma, or Helaman. It is primarily the work of Mormon, who did his work of compilation centuries after the prophets whose ministries make up most of the record. He created the book by drawing from documents written much earlier than his time. The narrative is for the most part in his words, but he quotes frequently from his sources, and the divisions of the book are named after the prophets whose original records he used. If we did not have the Words of Mormon, the books of Mormon and Moroni, and a few other hints, we would have an anonymous book compiled centuries after the events depicted in it.

Much of the Old Testament may have been composed in

that very way. With respect to Genesis, Moses may be the anonymous editor or author who compiled the book long after the events it recounts. On the other hand, he may be its original writer, and its final composition may be the work of others long after his time.

The record of Joseph Smith's prophetic ministry is a model of a different sort. The Doctrine and Covenants is a collection of revelations (almost all to Joseph Smith) presented without context except for brief introductions supplied by modern editors. During the Prophet's lifetime, editions were published in 1833 (the Book of Commandments, 65 sections[5]), 1835 (103 sections), and 1844 (111 sections).[6] It was not until 1876, thirty-two years after Joseph Smith's death, that twenty-five more of his revelations were added to the book, and the last was not added until 1981, more than a century later. After his death in 1844, all of those revelations circulated separately until they were included by others in the canonical collection.

The Prophet attempted to provide context for the revelations by beginning the compilation of what was called then the "History of Joseph Smith." He commenced it in 1838 by dictating an account of his early experiences, to which the texts of the revelations were added.[7] The history was compiled by him and his clerks from available sources, including his memory, his journals, and the records of others. The publication began in 1842, with installments appearing periodically in the Church's newspaper, the *Times and Seasons*.[8]

At the Prophet's death, the history had been compiled to 1838 but was published only to 1831. The work continued, both in Nauvoo and eventually in Utah, where installments were published in the *Deseret News* until 1858.[9] Decades later, Elder B. H. Roberts compiled the history into six volumes, refining it with his own careful editorial hand. It was published as *History of The Church of Jesus Christ of Latter-day Saints,* by Joseph Smith.[10] It is still in print today, and it remains an important historical record.

But did Joseph Smith write it? The *History of the Church* starts with autobiographical material that the Prophet dictated to scribes. It then shifts to the format of an ongoing diary, with his journals providing the framework. Although he kept intermittent journals during the 1830s, the information for that decade is not as complete as it is for the 1840s, when his clerks kept a record of his life. Some journal entries appear to have been dictated by the Prophet, but much of the journal material was kept independently by his clerks, who recorded his daily activities as they observed them, sometimes in the first person. In the compilation of his history, clerks' entries in the third person were transformed to first person, making the Prophet the speaker. Where there were gaps in the record, passages from the journals of other Church members were added to supply the needed information so none of the significant documented acts or words of Joseph Smith would be excluded, regardless of the source.[11] Letters, transcriptions of sermons, and other documents were added in their proper sequence to make the record as complete as possible. Although these procedures may seem odd to some modern readers, they were in keeping with the practice of nineteenth-century historiography. By today's definitions, we would not say that Joseph Smith "wrote" the *History of the Church,* but it was clearly created at his instruction and under his direction, and the historians who continued the process after his death were completing the work he had begun.

In 1938 Elder Joseph Fielding Smith of the Quorum of the Twelve Apostles published *Teachings of the Prophet Joseph Smith,* a collection of the Prophet's writings and sermons, mostly extracted from the *History of the Church.*[12] Because this book was intended to be a compilation of Joseph Smith's words, the Prophet is listed as its author, even though he did not compile it and probably never thought of publishing such a book—and it first came out more than ninety years after his death. Similarly, in 1994, when I published *Joseph Smith's Commentary on the Bible,* a collection of excerpts from primary records of his sermons and writings, the United States Library of Congress cataloged it with Joseph Smith as its author—150 years after his death—and with me in the supporting role of compiler and editor.[13]

The relevance of these examples to the authorship of Genesis is that they illustrate how complicated the question of authorship can be even for a fairly recent historical figure such as Joseph Smith. Although it is my view that Genesis comes from Moses, we cannot say whether or to what extent he wrote it himself, dictated it to scribes, or assigned others to write or compile it in his name. Nor do we know whether he possessed earlier documents from which he worked. We also do not know what happened to his text after his time.

MOSES AND GENESIS

Genesis is clearly not the primary record of Adam, Enoch, Noah, or Melchizedek. Those records were undoubtedly written, but they have not yet been revealed to us. Genesis is merely an overview intended to preface the record of ancient Israel, the Old Testament. As Moses produced the book, he may have quoted or summarized parts of it from earlier documents available to him. Other parts of the book were probably given him by revelation. Perhaps earlier documents came into Moses' hands by having been passed down through an Israelite family in Egypt or through the family of Moses' father-in-law, Jethro, a descendant of Abraham.[14]

It seems likely that the original language of Moses' book of Genesis was Egyptian. Egyptian was his native tongue, because he had been reared in an Egyptian home, and God speaks to his servants "after the manner of their language" (D&C 1:24), just as he did later with Nephi and later still with Joseph Smith. The scribes Moses employed to assist him in his duties were probably trained only in Egyptian. It is possible that the Israelites in Egypt were still speaking a West Semitic language like that of their ancestors centuries earlier in Canaan. If they were, we have no evidence that their language existed in written form, in a time when very few people—for the most part only professional scribes—were literate. Biblical Hebrew, the language of the book of Genesis today, did not even exist in Moses' time and only evolved later after the Israelites were settled in Canaan. If the Mosaic record in the Pentateuch was written in Egyptian, that might explain King Benjamin's enigmatic statement that Lehi was able to read the plates of brass because he knew that language (see Mosiah 1:4).[15]

Aside from the accounts in the first few chapters of Genesis, which were revealed before the deliverance of Israel from Egypt (see Moses 1:26), we do not know at what point in Moses' career the Genesis material was made known to him and his people. But ancient Israel's profound need for Genesis should be clear to all who read it. The Israelites in Moses' day were experiencing both a rebirth as a nation and a restoration of revealed truth. The information contained in Genesis was vital for their establishment as a covenant people and for their relocation to the land that had been promised them through their forefathers. Genesis taught Moses' people who they were, where they came from, and where they were going. It taught them of the one true God, in whose image they were created, who personally cares about his children and takes an active interest in their activities. It made clear to them that they were the inheritors of sacred covenants God had made with the good men and women from whom they descended. And it let them know that the land to which they were being led was theirs.

Based on clues in the Hebrew text, some scholars believe that Genesis in its current form dates to centuries after the time of Moses in the social and political setting of the Israelite monarchy, or even later. A theory of the composition of Genesis that first gained popularity in the nineteenth century is called the Documentary Hypothesis. It asserts that Genesis as we have it now was created when three earlier records were joined into one.[16] Many scholars have since abandoned this theory, but the search goes on for a coherent explanation of how Genesis was compiled.[17] Unfortunately, we cannot trace the history of the text after the time of Moses. It is not impossible that different versions of Moses' writings developed over time and circulated independently, to be woven together by an editor in a later period. But this is not necessarily the best explanation. We do not know to what degree Moses' Genesis text was influenced by later hands—some inspired and some with less inspiration and authority.[18] And again, our current Hebrew Genesis is likely a translation from something earlier.

Thanks to the latter-day restoration of the gospel, we now have a better understanding of Genesis than has been available to the world in general since Old Testament times. In the Joseph Smith Translation, the Prophet made far more changes in Genesis than in any other book. The book of Abraham adds even more to our understanding of the era of Genesis, as do important revelations in the Book of Mormon, the Doctrine and Covenants, and the sermons and writings of Joseph Smith.

Although we do not know how much of the truth thus restored was in the original book of Genesis, we can say that the Restoration has brought to our knowledge a much clearer understanding of the fundamental principles of Genesis and the keys to comprehending its history and teachings. In the Church today we recognize our role as modern Israel partly because of the book of Genesis, which is as vital to our own understanding as it was to the understanding of our spiritual and lineal forebears of ancient times. Indeed, it is not insignificant that the modern-day restoration of true religion also embodied the restoration of much of the foundational material that is part of the Genesis history.

NOTES

1. An interesting and fairly comprehensive discussion of the authorship question of Genesis is found in Victor P. Hamilton, *The Book of Genesis Chapters 1–17*, New International Commentary on the Old Testament series (Grand Rapids, Mich.: Eerdmans, 1990), 11–38.

2. Some other examples include Joshua 1:7–8; 23:6; 1 Kings 2:3; 2 Kings 14:6; 23:25; 2 Chronicles 23:18; 25:4; 35:12; Ezra 3:2; 6:18; Nehemiah 13:1; and Daniel 9:11, 13.

3. Some other examples include Mark 12:19; Luke 20:28; John 1:45; Acts 28:23; and 1 Corinthians 9:9.

4. Or perhaps the "five books of Moses" correspond only with our Genesis.

5. Called "chapters" in the Book of Commandments.

6. The 1844 edition was prepared during the Prophet's lifetime but came off the press after his death.

7. The earliest narratives are found in Dean C. Jessee, ed., *Autobiographical and Historical Writings*, vol. 1 of *The Papers of Joseph Smith* series (Salt Lake City: Deseret Book, 1989–).

8. See "History of Joseph Smith," *Times and Seasons*, 15 March 1842, 726–28.

9. See Dean C. Jessee, "The Writing of Joseph Smith's History," *BYU Studies* 11, no. 4 (summer 1971): 439–73.

10. Joseph Smith, *History of The Church of Jesus Christ of Latter-day Saints,* ed. B. H. Roberts (Salt Lake City: Deseret News, 1902–12). A seventh volume dealing with events after the death of Joseph Smith was published in 1932.

11. Perhaps the most famous such passage comes from the diary of Wilford Woodruff, recorded 28 November 1841: "I spent the day at B. Young in company with Joseph & the Twelve in conversing upon a variety of Subjects. . . . Joseph Said the Book of Mormon was the most correct of any Book on Earth & the key stone of our religion & a man would get nearer to God by abiding by its precepts than any other Book." Scott G. Kenney, ed., *Wilford Woodruff's Journal 1833–1898 Typescript* (Midvale, Utah: Signature Books, 1983), 2:139.

12. Joseph Smith, *Teachings of the Prophet Joseph Smith,* sel. Joseph Fielding Smith (Salt Lake City: Deseret Book, 1938).

13. Joseph Smith, *Joseph Smith's Commentary on the Bible,* comp. and ed. Kent P. Jackson (Salt Lake City: Deseret Book, 1994), copyright page.

14. I thank my colleague Terrence L. Szink for this excellent suggestion.

15. I this is true, it seems likely that *only* the Pentateuch would have been written in Egyptian.

16. See E. A. Speiser, *Genesis,* Anchor Bible 1 (Garden City, N.Y.: Doubleday, 1964), xxii–xxxvii. Some more recent revisionists want to date Genesis as late as the Persian period.

17. See the discussion in Hamilton, *Book of Genesis,* 11–38.

18. An example of words in Genesis written after Moses' time is the place name *Dan* in Genesis 14:14: Abraham "pursued [the kings] unto Dan." Dan was Abraham's great-grandson. The place was named after his descendants when they took possession of it long after the time of Moses, an event recorded in Judges 18:29.

6

THE CREATION

I N 1982 ELDER BRUCE R. MCCONKIE of the Quorum of the Twelve Apostles reminded us: "Our analysis properly begins with the frank recital that our knowledge about the Creation is limited. We do not know the how and why and when of all things. Our finite limitations are such that we could not comprehend them if they were revealed to us in all their glory, fulness, and perfection. What has been revealed is that portion of the Lord's eternal word which we must believe and understand if we are to envision the truth about the Fall and the Atonement and thus become heirs of salvation. This is all we are obligated to know in our day."[1] Indeed, there are many questions about the Creation for which the Lord has not given us answers. Faithful Latter-day Saints, even having been blessed with what we know through modern revelation, need to be satisfied for now not knowing all things.

REVEALED ACCOUNTS

In the Church we have four revealed accounts of the Creation, three of which are in the scriptures.

Genesis 1 and 2. The account in Genesis 1 and 2 is in Moses' words, describing things shown him in vision. Moses is the speaker, and God is discussed in the third person: "In the beginning God created the heaven and the earth. . . . And God said, Let there be light: and there was light" (Gen. 1:1, 3). The Old Testament tells us nothing of the origin of the biblical Creation account, or even of its authorship. Latter-day Saints can attribute it to Moses because of important information in the Joseph Smith Translation of the Bible.

Moses 2 and 3. The Joseph Smith Translation of the Genesis account is now in Moses 2 and 3 in the Pearl of Great Price. It was revealed to the Prophet Joseph Smith sometime in the summer or fall of 1830. God, not Moses, is the speaker, and Moses is quoting God's words. "Yea, in the beginning I created the heaven, and the earth. . . . And I, God, said: Let there be light; and there was light" (Moses 2:1, 3). We know of the Mosaic authorship of this record (and hence also of Genesis 1–2) because it is preceded by a great vision in which God appeared to Moses and showed him his creative works (see Moses 1). God told Moses that he had created "worlds without number" and that he had created them by his Only Begotten Son (Moses 1:33; see also v. 32). But "only an account of this earth, and the inhabitants thereof" would the Lord make known to Moses (Moses 1:35). "And now, Moses, my son, I will speak unto thee concerning this earth upon which thou standest; and thou shalt write the things which I shall speak" (Moses 1:40). "Behold, I reveal unto you concerning this heaven, and this earth; write the words which I speak. . . . Yea, in the beginning I created the heaven, and the earth" (Moses 2:1). The Creation account then follows.

The Joseph Smith Translation account differs from the Genesis account in several instances. Most of the changes made by Joseph Smith are rather small, but among the most important is the emphasis that Jesus Christ was present at the Creation, working with the Father. To Genesis 1:5 is added "And this I did by the word of my power," referring to Christ as the Creator (Moses 2:5). Later in the chapter, "And God said" is replaced with "And I, God, said unto mine Only Begotten, which was with me from the beginning" (Moses 2:26; see also v. 27). Other small insertions of words make the text more clear (e.g., Moses 2:16, 18).

Abraham 4 and 5. Like the account in the book of Moses, the account in the book of Abraham is also in the Pearl of Great Price. It is related in the words of Abraham, describing the work of the creating Gods: "And they went down at the beginning, and they, that is the Gods, organized and formed the heavens and the earth. . . . And they (the Gods) said: Let there be light; and there was light" (Abr. 4:1, 3). Because this is an account of works yet to be accomplished, a planning session (see Abr. 4:31; 5:3–4), President Joseph Fielding Smith called it the "blueprint" of the Creation.[2]

The temple. In the temple we also learn of the Creation, as our Church leaders have taught.[3]

DAYS OF THE CREATION

In the scriptural accounts, we are taught of God's creative work of six days. "But first," Elder McConkie asked, "what is a day? It is a specified time period; it is an age, an eon, a division of eternity; it is the time between two identifiable events." The vagueness in this definition is deliberate, as are the words Elder McConkie chose to discuss the length of the days: "Each day, of whatever length, has the duration needed for its purposes." Moreover, "there is no revealed recitation specifying that each of the 'six days' involved in the Creation was of the same duration."[4]

Convenient for our discussion is that the verse numbers for the days are the same in each of the three scriptural Creation accounts.

Day 1: The heaven and the earth; light (vv. 1–5). The Joseph Smith Translation account emphasizes that our scriptural record pertains only to our own earth and its environment in the cosmos: "Behold, I reveal unto you concerning *this* heaven, and *this* earth. . . . Yea, in the beginning I created the heaven, and *the earth upon which thou standest*" (Moses 2:1; emphasis added). When first formed, the earth "was empty and desolate, because [the Gods] had not formed anything but the earth" (Abr. 4:2). God said, "Let there be light; and there was light" (Moses 2:3), a light that was both "bright" (Abr. 4:4) and "good" (Moses 2:4). The light created on the first day must be something different from the daylight of the fourth day that resulted from the earth's position relative to the sun. The light of the first day appears to be primal light with which the Creation begins. Perhaps it was, as scientists describe, a "Big Bang" in which pure energy exploded into an expanding cosmic fireball where energy was converted into clouds of gas and matter and eventually into galaxies, stars, and planets. The initial burst of divine power with which the Creation began still burns today as it illuminates the trillions of stars and galaxies and provides the energy for every molecule of matter. All of these bear testimony to God's creative majesty, because "the elements are the tabernacle of God" (D&C 93:35). Modern revelation speaks of the light of Christ which "proceedeth forth from the presence of God to fill the immensity of space" (D&C 88:12). Christ is "in all and through all things, the light of truth" (D&C 88:6), and his light illuminates the sun, the moon, the stars, and even us (see D&C 88:7–11). His is the light "which is in all things, which giveth life to all things, which is the law by which all things are governed, even the power of God who sitteth upon his throne, who is in the bosom of eternity, who is in the midst of all things" (D&C 88:13).

Day 2: Atmosphere (vv. 6–8). The King James Version word *firmament* translates a Hebrew word that means a "stretching out." The book of Abraham word *expanse* represents the original word better. This expanse separated the waters on the surface of the earth from the waters above—or, ocean water from atmospheric water, or clouds. In the image of the scriptures, the waters above the expanse remained in place until the Flood, when the "windows of heaven were opened" and it rained for forty days and forty nights (Gen. 7:11; see also v. 12).

Day 3: Ocean; continent; plant life (vv. 9–13). The wording suggests the creation of one continent and one body of ocean water at this early stage of the earth's history. Regarding the beginning of plant life on earth, the Abrahamic record is the clearest and most explicit: "And the Gods organized the earth to bring forth grass from its own seed, and the herb to bring forth herb from its own seed, yielding seed after his kind; and the earth to bring forth the tree from its own seed, yielding fruit, whose seed could only bring forth the same in itself, after his kind" (Abr. 4:12). The biological principle set in place on the third day is fundamental to all life on earth, both to plants and to animals. Joseph Smith called it "a decree of the Lord": living things yield seed to propagate their kind, and each comes forth only from its own species "and cannot come forth after any other law or principle."[5]

Day 4: The sun, the moon, and the stars; earth's revolutions and rotations (vv. 14–19). On the fourth day, the earth was set in its place relative to the sun, the moon, and the visible stars.

The earth's revolutions and rotations were also established. The "lights in the expanse of the heaven" (Abr. 4:14) would not only provide energy and light for the earth but also determine how we measure time (v. 14). We measure a day as one rotation of the earth on its axis. A year is one revolution of the earth around the sun. Our seasons are determined by the angle of the earth in its revolutions. A month originally represented a revolution of the moon around the earth. The stars are signs that show directions in the night—the Southern Cross indicates south, and the Big Dipper and the North Star indicate north. The sun would rule the day, and the moon and the stars would rule the night (see Abr. 4:16). Joseph Smith taught: "God set the sun, the moon, and the stars in the heavens and gave them their laws, conditions, and bounds which they cannot pass except by his command. They all move in perfect harmony in their sphere and order and are as wonders, lights, and signs unto us."[6] These cycles of days, seasons, and years are more important than we sometimes realize. The distinction between night and day, for example, is fundamental. Humans, most animals, and many plants have biological rhythms that are connected to the alternating cycles of day and night. And the year determines the reproductive schedules and even lifetimes of many forms of life.

Day 5: Water animals; birds (vv. 20–23). The beginning of animal life on earth came about when the Gods commanded, or prepared (see Abr. 4:21), the waters to bring forth life "abundantly" (vv. 20, 21). From the waters were created two broad categories of animals—sea creatures and birds. These were the first to receive a commandment: they were to "be fruitful," to "multiply," to "fill the waters," and to "multiply in the earth" (v. 22).

Day 6: Land animals; humans (vv. 24–31). Next the earth

brought forth, in response to divine command, land animals. These are characterized in broad categories. "Cattle" is used to translate a Hebrew word that refers to large domesticated animals; "creeping things" suggests smaller animals in many varieties; and "beasts of the earth" is used to translate a word that refers to large nondomestic animals. The command for these animals to be fruitful and multiply is not recorded in the scriptural accounts, but the words "after their kind" (vv. 24–25) suggest that the divine mandate to reproduce was in effect.

The crowning act of God's work on the sixth day was the creation of humans. As God's children, whose eternal life was the Father's work and glory (see Moses 1:39), they were the primary reason for which the earth and all that is on it were created. Only when humans were in place was the work of the Creation complete.

OUT OF NOTHING

In his sermons and writings, the Prophet Joseph Smith provided inspired insights into the Creation.[7] He taught: "Learned doctors tell us God created the heavens and earth out of nothing. They account it blasphemy to contradict the idea. They will call you a fool. You ask them why. They say, 'Doesn't the Bible say he created the world?' And they infer that it must be out of nothing."[8] This is the doctrine of *ex nihilo* creation—"creation out of nothing." It is a fundamental belief of traditional Christianity that is based on the idea that God cannot need or lack anything. If God needed preexisting materials to create from, it would mean that he is insufficient and not all-powerful, and therefore not God. But Joseph Smith taught: "God did not make the earth out of nothing, for it is contrary to a rational mind and reason that a something could be brought from a nothing. Also, it is contrary to the principle and means by which God does work."⁹ "This earth was organized or formed out of other planets which were broken up and remodeled and made into the one on which we live. The elements are eternal."¹⁰ That the Prophet was referring not to large portions of other earths but to recycled elements is clear: "The word *create* came from the word *bārā'*. [It] doesn't mean so; it means to organize, same as [a] man would use to build a ship. Hence we infer that God had materials to organize from—chaos, chaotic matter. Element had an existence from the time [God] had. The pure principles of element are principles that never can be destroyed; they may be organized and reorganized, but not destroyed."¹¹ Modern scientists agree with Joseph Smith, who articulated what they now call the principle of the "conservation of matter and energy." Matter can be converted into energy or into other forms of matter. It can be "organized and reorganized," but it cannot be created out of nothing, and it cannot be destroyed.

VERY GOOD

The Creation was not a chance occurrence or a random product of nature. It was a deliberate work accomplished at God's command and fulfilled under his direction: "And I, God, said: Let there be light; and there was light" (Moses 2:3). "And I, God, said: Let there be dry land; and it was so" (Moses 2:9). "And I, God, said: Let the earth bring forth the living creature. . . . And it was so" (Moses 2:24). Modern revelation emphasizes this principle, adding phrases such as "and it was so, even as I spake" (Moses 2:6; see also vv. 5, 7, 16), and "and it was so, even as they ordered" (Abr. 4:7; see also vv. 9, 11). After the commands were given for the creative activities, "the Gods watched those things which they had ordered until they obeyed" (Abr. 4:18; see also vv. 10, 12). This watching "until they obeyed" suggests that the Creators were not spectators but oversaw the process or saw to it that the elements obeyed. Thus they were not surprised to observe that what they had created was "good."

After most of the events in the Creation, God assessed his work and pronounced it "good" (Moses 2:4, 10, 12, 18, 21, 25). The Joseph Smith Translation teaches that this judgment was not only an evaluation of each day's activity but a cumulative assessment of the continuing process. For example, after the fourth day God said, "And I, God, saw that all things which I had made were good" (Moses 2:18).

After the end of the Creation, following the work of the sixth day, God used different language to evaluate his accomplishments: "And I, God, saw everything that I had made, and, behold, *all things* which I had made were *very good*" (Moses 2:31; emphasis added). It was not until humans were on the earth that it and everything on it were pronounced "very good." But this assessment implies more than simply the presence of Adam and Eve. Elsewhere we learn that when the Creation was finished and Adam and Eve were placed on the earth, the earth was "spiritual," a term that describes its nature prior to the time when it became "fallen" and "natural." "All things were before created; but *spiritually* were they created and made according to my word" (Moses 3:7; emphasis added). After the Creation, all things were "spiritual" until the Fall. They were indeed physical, material, and tangible, but they were spiritual in the sense that they were unfallen, immortal, in harmony with divine order, and not yet subject to decay and corruption and to what we observe as the laws of nature. "For it was spiritual in the day that I created it; for it remaineth in the sphere in which I, God, created it, yea, even all things which I prepared for the use of man" (Moses 3:9). This pure condition is suggested in the words "very good." Before the Fall, things were spiritual in the same way that people will be spiritual when they are resurrected, when "they can die no more; their spirits uniting with their bodies, never to be divided; thus the whole becoming *spiritual* and immortal, that they can no more see corruption" (Alma 11:45; emphasis added).[12]

DINOSAURS AND OTHER LIVING THINGS

In the surface of the earth, the Lord has given us a record of his creative activity here since the beginning, showing his careful hand at work in preparing our planet to receive his children. This account of the Creation is often difficult to understand. In the Millennium we will comprehend it better, for we are promised that when Christ returns he will reveal "things that are above, and things that are beneath, things that are in the earth, and upon the earth" (D&C 101:34). In the earth's crust we see a succession of layers that show evidence of the progression of time. The bottom layers are the most ancient, the top the most recent. In the record of those layers, we see evidence that when the earth was first formed, there was no life on it. But over the course of time and as the Lord commanded, the earth brought forth life—first plants and then animals, the complexity of the organisms increasing with the passage of time. Among the early inhabitants of our planet were the dinosaurs, not the only but certainly the most well-known of prehistoric life. Where do they fit into the earth's history? As Brigham Young University paleontologist James A. Jensen summarized, "It is very simple. The dinosaurs were real. They lived here on the earth sometime during the time the earth was being prepared for us."[13]

The scriptures teach that when Adam and Eve were placed on the earth they were immortal, living in a state of paradise (see 2 Ne. 2:22; Moses 3:17). They, and apparently also the plants and animals, were not subject to death, which came when our first parents transgressed divine law and brought about the Fall. But how do we harmonize fossil remains that record the deaths of millions of prehistoric plants and animals with the scriptural evidence that there was no death on earth until the Fall? The simplest answer is perhaps correct: It appears that during the time the earth was being created, there was death on earth. The life cycles of plants and animals, including their deaths, were part of the Creation, part of the means by which God prepared the earth for us. During the six days, God made the earth ready for the human family. Anticipating our needs, he set in place everything that would be required for our existence and our well-being. He created the atmosphere we would need to breathe and the plants and animals we would need to sustain our lives. The geological record tells us that he created great forests, teeming with wildlife of every variety, whose plants and animals over the course of time would live, die, decay, and be transformed into the coal and oil reserves that now power our world. God's preparation of this resource would enable us to have light in our homes and churches, printed scriptures in our hands, and fresh food on our tables. And this same power source would enable Church leaders and missionaries to travel through the earth bearing the message of the gospel. All of these blessings required that other forms of life be created before us, each with its role in the process, each fulfilling the intent for which God placed it here.

Latter-day Saint scripture makes it clear that when Christ

comes again the earth will be transformed from its present fallen state into a state of paradise in which there will again be no death (see D&C 101:29). The earth will be glorified to endure God's presence and will be "renewed," meaning made new again, and restored to its "paradisiacal glory," meaning made again as it was before the Fall (A of F 10). This will happen not as a natural development in the earth's biology but as a sudden, dramatic intervention of divine power to supersede the course of nature. In a like way, it seems probable that when the Creation had progressed to the point the earth was ready for Adam and Eve, a similar dramatic transition took place that glorified it and transformed it from its developing condition into a state of paradise in which there was no death. God intervened in the course of his natural creative process to change the earth so it would be a proper home for the beginnings of human history. It was made "spiritual," or "very good." He called it Eden and placed in it a man and a woman, Adam and Eve. Later, the fall of our first parents caused the fall of the earth and of all that was in it. The Fall brought death into our world, and the condition of paradise was withdrawn. Since geological evidence records only death, not life, no trace of Eden would remain once it had ceased to exist, no matter how long it lasted.

NOTES

1. Bruce R. McConkie, "Christ and the Creation," *Ensign*, June 1982, 10.

2. Joseph Fielding Smith, *Doctrines of Salvation*, comp. Bruce R. McConkie, 3 vols. (Salt Lake City: Bookcraft, 1954–56), 1:75. Perhaps the planning ends at Abraham 5:3 and the actual creating begins at Abraham 5:4.

3. McConkie, "Christ and the Creation," 11; Smith, *Doctrines of Salvation*, 1:75.

4. McConkie, "Christ and the Creation," 11.

5. Andrew F. Ehat and Lyndon W. Cook, eds., *The Words of Joseph Smith: The Contemporary Accounts of the Nauvoo Discourses of the Prophet Joseph* (Provo, Utah: Religious Studies Center, Brigham Young University, 1980), 107.

6. Ibid.; spelling, capitalization, and punctuation standardized.

7. See Joseph Smith, *Joseph Smith's Commentary on the Bible,* comp. and ed. Kent P. Jackson (Salt Lake City: Deseret Book, 1994), 1–11.

8. Ehat and Cook, eds., *Words of Joseph Smith,* 359; spelling, capitalization, and punctuation standardized.

9. Ibid., 61; spelling, capitalization, and punctuation standardized.

10. Ibid., 60; spelling standardized.

11. Ibid., 359; spelling, capitalization, and punctuation standardized.

12. See also McConkie, "Christ and the Creation," 13–15.

13. Remarks to Brigham Young University Religious Instruction faculty, 24 October 1980; transcript in my possession.

7

ADAM AND EVE

"WHAT WAS THE DESIGN OF THE ALMIGHTY in making man? It was to exalt him to be as God."[1] Through modern revelation we know who we are, where we came from, and where we will go after this life. But as for how we were created, the Lord has chosen to reveal little.

The accounts of human creation are brief, simplified, and at least to some extent symbolic—although we do not always know what is symbolic and what is not. The account in Genesis 2:7 depicts God *forming* man from the ground. The King James Version word *form* translates a Hebrew word used to describe the work of a potter making a vessel from clay. Some early Church leaders expressed reservations about our creation being like that of a potter and his handiwork.[2] Some believers in the Bible, including some Latter-day Saints, view evolution as a process whereby God created, developed, and differentiated life on earth. In doing so, they reject the beliefs of modern scientists generally that the process had no guiding hand and no divine plan.[3] With the grand design of "worlds without number" in mind

(Moses 1:33), some Latter-day Saints have suggested that Adam and Eve were born of parents elsewhere and brought to this earth when it was ready for them[4] or that they were born of heavenly parents here.[5]

For all of these beliefs, President Spencer W. Kimball reminded us: "We don't know exactly how their coming into this world happened, and when we're able to understand it the Lord will tell us."[6] Clearly there are limitations on what God is willing to make known to us at this time. When Moses desired to know more about God's creations than God wanted to reveal, the prophet received a response that is still timely today: "For mine own purpose have I made these things. Here is wisdom and it remaineth in me" (Moses 1:31).

The intent of these words is clear: God knows what he is doing, but he does not always share with us what he knows and what he does. What has been revealed of our Creation is not scientific detail about how it was accomplished. Instead, the Lord has provided broad images sufficient to help us understand the Creation in a *doctrinal* context. The Creation is the backdrop for the Fall and the Atonement, and the Lord has revealed only enough about it so we can understand those other fundamentals. During the Millennium our questions will be answered: "In that day when the Lord shall come, he shall reveal all things—things which have passed, and hidden things which no man knew, things of the earth, by which it was made, and the purpose and the end thereof" (D&C 101:32–33).

THE UNIQUENESS OF HUMANS

The accounts of the creation of humans (see Gen. 1:26–28; Moses 2:26–28; Abr. 4:26–28) leave no doubt that we are unique among all God's creatures. We see this in at least three ways.

First, humans are created in God's image: "And I, God, said unto mine Only Begotten, which was with me from the beginning: Let us make man in our image, after our likeness. . . . And I, God, created man in mine own image, in the image of mine Only Begotten created I him" (Moses 2:26–27; cf. Abr. 4:26–27). Traditional Christianity rejects a literal interpretation of the Genesis statement that man is created in God's image (see Gen. 1:26–27). But the words in the biblical account are meant to be taken at face value. The terms *image* and *likeness* are correct translations of the Hebrew words *ṣelem* and *děmût*. The first of these is used mostly for statues and other representative images. The second is based on a verb that means to "look like" or "be like." An ancient statue of a king of Syria contains an inscription with the same two words, both referring to the statue.[7] This shows that the words mean a literal, recognizable likeness of the king, just as in Genesis they mean that man is a literal, recognizable likeness of God. Similarly, the Bible tells us that Adam later "begat a son in his own likeness, after his image" (Gen. 5:3). Joseph Smith taught: "God himself, who sits enthroned in yonder heavens, is a man like unto one of yourselves. . . . If you were to see him today you would see him a man. For Adam was a man in fashion and image like unto him."[8]

Second, God gave humans dominion over the rest of his creations. Man's stewardship extends not only to the plants and animals but to the earth itself (see Moses 2:26).

Third, God was more directly involved in the creation of humans than in the creation of other things. Notice the carefully chosen language for the origin of plants and animals: "Let the earth bring forth grass. . . . And the earth brought forth grass" (Moses 2:11–12). "Let the waters bring forth abundantly the moving creature . . . which the waters brought forth abundantly" (Moses 2:20–21). And "Let the earth bring forth the living creature" (Moses 2:24). Plants and animals were created when God commanded the earth and the sea to bring them forth. But the process of human creation is depicted in strikingly different terms: "Let us make man. . . . And I, God, created man" (Moses 2:26–27). The Abraham account is even more to the point: "Let us go down and form man. . . . So the Gods went down to organize man" (Abr. 4:26–27). Whatever the process for creating humans may have been, the scriptures are clear in differentiating between that process and the process by which other life was made.

ADAM

The creation of humans is both the high point and the final act of God's labors in the Creation accounts. It was after their creation that God ceased and rested from his work (see Moses 3:1–2). From that point on, the scriptures become a record of the human family, and the other things God created play a role only insofar as humans interact with them. This emphasis shows that our first parents, Adam and Eve, along with their posterity to the end of time, were the fundamental reason for God's creative work on earth. The scriptures give us two separate narratives for the creation of Adam and Eve. The first is in the narrative of the six days—in Genesis 1, Moses 2, and Abraham 4. The second is in the chapters of Genesis, Moses, and Abraham that follow. There we have an account of man's formation from the earth (see Gen. 2:7; Moses 3:7; Abr. 5:7) and a separate account of the creation of Eve (see Gen. 2:18, 21–25; Moses 3:18, 21–25; Abr. 5:14–19).

In the scriptures we read that God "formed man from the dust of the ground" (Moses 3:7; Abr. 5:7). Adam learned that he would eat of the ground all the days of his life (see Moses 4:23), and the Lord told him: "Thou shalt return unto the ground . . . for out of it wast thou taken" (Moses 4:25). In the accounts of Adam's creation, his connection to the soil of the earth is shown not only in these verses but also in his name. The Hebrew noun *'ādām,* meaning "man" and rendered "Adam" frequently in the King James translation, comes from the same root as *'ădāmâ,* the word for *ground, soil,* or *earth.* Adam's name, "Man," is the masculine form, and *'ădāmâ* is the feminine. The *'ādām* was made from the *'ădāmâ,* showing the close relationship between humanity and "Mother Earth." Adam's name, therefore, means something like "Ground Man," "Soil Man," or "Earth Man."

But the elements of the earth would not be the only component in Adam's creation. After the Gods formed man from the ground, they "took his spirit (that is, the man's spirit), and put it into him." Next a divine act brought the body-spirit combination to life: the Gods "breathed into his nostrils the breath of life," by which "man became a living soul" (Abr. 5:7). Joseph Smith taught: "When God breathed into man's nostrils he became a living soul. Before that he did not live, and when that was taken away his body died."[9] "God made man and put into it Adam's spirit,"[10] and "God made a tabernacle and put a spirit in it, and it became a human soul."[11]

The Hebrew word *'ādām* means *man* in the generic sense—*human* rather than *male.* While these verses represent the creation of an actual, historical man, they also represent the creation of the woman and the whole human family, because the pronouns and verbal conjugations regarding the *'ādām* are almost always plural.[12] "And I, God, created man in mine own image, in the image of mine Only Begotten created I him; male and female created I them" (Moses 2:27). There is a progression in this verse from "him" to "them" and from "the man" to "male and female," showing that what is being described is the creation of both Adam and Eve. President Spencer W. Kimball stated that the man created here was "not a separate man, but a complete man, which is husband and wife."[13] Moreover, "in the day that God created man, in the likeness of God made he him; in the image of his own body, male and female, created he them, and blessed them, and called their name Adam" (Moses 6:8–9).

EVE

The scriptures highlight Eve's beginnings with the account of her creation from one of Adam's ribs. The Hebrew text at Genesis 2:22 says: "And the Lord God made the rib . . . into a woman." Although the story's language is certainly figurative,[14] the words are deliberately chosen to teach more than what is seen on the surface. Of all the Lord's earthly creations the woman is unique, because everything else—the man included—was created out of the ground. But she was made out of the man—from part of his body that was removed for the very purpose of making her. The symbolism was not lost on Adam. He recognized that the woman was his flesh and bone in a real way. They belonged to and with each other because neither was whole alone. A part of the man was missing that could only be recovered with the woman at his side, so he sensed instinctively his incompleteness, just as she had a natural desire to be with him (see Moses 4:22). Because of his sense of incompleteness, a man will willingly leave his parents to join with his wife. Since collectively they are *'ādām,* and separately they are less than whole, it is only when they are together that they add up to "one flesh." Even the location of the rib plays a role in the imagery of this oneness. Sister Patricia T. Holland stated: "The scriptures indicate that God had figuratively taken a rib from Adam's side to make Eve, not from his front that she should lead him and not from his back that she should despise him, but from his side, under his arm, close to his heart. There, bone of his bone and flesh of his flesh, husband and wife were to be united in every way, side by side."[15]

Joseph Smith taught that Adam and Eve were not merely fellow sojourners in the Garden of Eden. They were a married couple, and God performed the ordinance: "[Marriage is] an institution of heaven, first solemnized in the garden of Eden by God himself, by the authority of everlasting priesthood."[16] Though they were naked, they were not ashamed in the privacy of their new home, and their eyes were not yet opened (see Moses 3:25; 4:13).

"And Adam called his wife's name Eve, because she was the mother of all living" (Moses 4:26). The woman's name does not mean "mother of all living," but it was given her because she would fill that role. Her name—*ḥawwâ* in Hebrew—is a unique feminine word that most likely comes from an archaic root for the verb *live*. The spelling in the Hebrew Bible suggests an intensive or facilitating meaning, hence something like "Life-Giver."[17]

ADAM, THE PRIESTHOOD, AND REVELATION

The Prophet Joseph Smith taught concerning Adam's importance in the priesthood: "Christ is the Great High priest; Adam next."[18]

"The priesthood was first given to Adam; he obtained the

first presidency and held the keys of it from generation to generation. He obtained it in the creation before the world was formed. . . . He had dominion given him over every living creature. He is Michael, the archangel spoken of in the scriptures. . . .

"The priesthood is an everlasting principle and existed with God from eternity and will to eternity, without beginning of days or end of years. The keys have to be brought from heaven whenever the gospel is sent. When they are revealed from heaven, it is by Adam's authority. . . . The Father called all spirits before him at the creation of man and organized them. He (Adam) is the head; [he] was told to multiply. The keys were given to him and by him to others, and he will have to give an account of his stewardship, and they to him."[19]

Thus Adam, under Christ, presides over all the human family. "He was the first and father of all, not only by progeny, but he was the first to hold the spiritual blessings, to whom was made known the plan of ordinances for the salvation of his posterity unto the end, and to whom Christ was first revealed, and through whom Christ has been revealed from heaven and will continue to be revealed from henceforth. Adam holds the keys of the Dispensation of the Fulness of Times." Further, "the dispensation[s] of all the times have been and will be revealed through him from the beginning to Christ and from Christ to the end of all the dispensations."[20]

Notes

1. Andrew F. Ehat and Lyndon W. Cook, eds., *The Words of Joseph Smith: The Contemporary Accounts of the Nauvoo Discourses of the Prophet Joseph* (Provo, Utah: Religious Studies Center, Brigham Young University, 1980), 247; punctuation standardized.

2. E.g., *Journal of Discourses,* 26 vols. (London: Latter-day Saints'

Book Depot, 1855–86), 2:6–7; Parley P. Pratt, *Key to the Science of Theology,* 10th ed. (Salt Lake City: Deseret Book, 1948), 55.

    3. See Morris S. Petersen, "Earth," in Daniel H. Ludlow, ed., *Encyclopedia of Mormonism* (New York: Macmillan, 1992), 431–33; John L. Sorenson, "Origin of Man," *Encyclopedia of Mormonism,* 1053–54.

    4. E.g., Pratt, *Key to the Science of Theology,* 54–55; B. H. Roberts, *The Gospel: An Exposition of Its First Principles and Man's Relationship to Deity,* 11th ed. (Salt Lake City: Deseret Book, 1966), 268–69.

    5. E.g., *Journal of Discourses,* 4:218.

    6. Spencer W. Kimball, "The Blessings and Responsibilities of Womanhood," *Ensign,* March 1976, 72.

    7. Ali Abou-Assaf, Pierre Bordreuil, and Alan R. Millard, *La statue de Tell Fekherye et son inscription bilingue assyro-araméene* (Paris: Reserche sur les civilisations, 1982), 23–24.

    8. Ehat and Cook, eds., *Words of Joseph Smith,* 349; spelling, capitalization, and punctuation standardized.

    9. *Times and Seasons,* 1 April 1842, 746.

    10. Ehat and Cook, eds., *Words of Joseph Smith,* 352; spelling, capitalization, and punctuation standardized.

    11. Ibid., 346; spelling, capitalization, and punctuation standardized.

    12. "Let them" (Moses 2:26), "be fruitful," "multiply," "replenish," "subdue," and "have dominion" (all plural verbal conjugations in Hebrew, 2:28), and "you" (plural, 2:29).

    13. Kimball, "Blessings and Responsibilities of Womanhood," 71.

    14. Ibid.

    15. Patricia T. Holland, in Jeffrey R. Holland and Patricia T. Holland, *On Earth As It Is in Heaven* (Salt Lake City: Deseret Book, 1989), 107.

    16. Dean C. Jessee, ed., *Autobiographical and Historical Writings,* vol. 1 of *The Papers of Joseph Smith* series (Salt Lake City: Deseret Book, 1989–), 146.

    17. See the discussion and references in Victor P. Hamilton, *The Book of Genesis Chapters 1–17,* New International Commentary on the Old Testament series (Grand Rapids, Mich.: Eerdmans, 1990), 205–6.

    18. Ehat and Cook, eds., *Words of Joseph Smith,* 9.

    19. Ibid., 8–9; capitalization and punctuation standardized.

    20. Ibid., 38–39; capitalization standardized.

8

IN THE GARDEN OF EDEN

O UR EARTH IS NOT TODAY AS IT WAS when it was first created, nor is it now as it will be in its final condition. It has
its own cycle of existence by which it is being transformed from
raw "materials" (Abr. 3:24) to a "sanctified and immortal state"
(D&C 130:9). This transformation can be identified in six
stages.

Stage 1: The Creation. Our scriptural accounts are of the creation of the physical world on which we live. Until the Creation
was accomplished, the earth and the materials from which it
was made were *without form, void, unorganized,* and still in a
state of *chaos* (see Gen. 1:2).

Stage 2: The Garden of Eden. Some scriptures depict Eden
as a distinct place on earth from which Adam and Eve were
driven at the Fall (e.g., Moses 4:29, 31; 5:4). But because their
fall brought about the fall of all the earth (see 2 Ne. 2:22), it
seems best to consider the whole world, and not only part of
it, as being in an Edenic condition. After the Creation the earth
was no longer in the formative state that characterized it prior

to its completion. It was now *organized* and *very good*, synonymous terms that show that it was a state of *paradise*. Although the earth was *physical*, it was also *spiritual*, meaning it was pure, uncorrupted, and in harmony with God, just as we have "spiritual experiences" when we are in harmony with God. The Lord said, "It was spiritual in the day that I created it; for it remaineth in the sphere in which I, God, created it" (Moses 3:9).[1]

Stage 3: The Fall. The Fall was the transformation of the earth to its current condition, brought about by the actions of Adam and Eve.

Stage 4: The fallen world. The fall of our first parents caused a dramatic change in the earth. No longer was it a state of paradise, in which all things were organized and in harmony. No longer could it be described as "very good" or "spiritual." It was now *fallen*, having descended to a less holy condition. As opposed to being spiritual, it was now *natural*, meaning that the laws of nature we observe today were put into effect. In this fallen world we are subject to pain, disease, sorrow, disappointment, disability, and many other problems. But when we, our Heavenly Father's children, learned of the opportunity to come to this place with all its dangers, we shouted for joy (see Job 38:4–7), because we knew that only through the circumstances of earth life can we progress to our ultimate destiny.

Stage 5: The Millennium. When Jesus Christ returns, the earth will be changed miraculously from its natural and fallen state to a state similar in most ways to what it was like in Eden. The earth "will be renewed and receive its paradisiacal glory" (A of F 10). Again it will be *organized*, *very good*, and *spiritual*. The circumstances of the Fall will be reversed: sorrow and death, among other things, will be no more (see D&C 101:29).

Stage 6: The celestial earth. After the Millennium this earth will become the celestial kingdom. "For after it hath filled the measure of its creation, it shall be crowned with glory, even with the presence of God the Father; that bodies who are of the celestial kingdom may possess it forever and ever; for, for this intent was it made and created, and for this intent are they sanctified. . . . Wherefore, it shall be sanctified; . . . and the righteous shall inherit it" (D&C 88:19–20, 26; see also vv. 10–18; cf. 130:9).

THE FALL

In studying the experiences of Adam and Eve in the Garden of Eden, we should be guided by an awareness of three fundamental limitations to what we know:

1. We do not have a complete account.

2. We do not know what is figurative and what is literal.

3. We do not know how much Adam and Eve knew and understood.

Without these safeguards we can too easily draw conclusions that are not supported by scriptural evidence.

The Joseph Smith Translation account of the experience in Eden begins with a background revelation concerning Satan (see Moses 4:1–4). In it Moses was taught that Satan was with God in the premortal world, where Satan put forth an impossible campaign promise to save everyone. He rebelled and attempted to overthrow the Father and the Son, seeking God's honor and power. Thus "he became Satan, yea, even the devil, the father of all lies, to deceive and to blind men, and to lead them captive at his will" (Moses 4:4). This introduction is meant to help us understand who our adversary was in the Garden and to warn us against believing anything he said there or anything he wants us to believe now. The Joseph Smith Translation includes an important addition that in desiring to beguile Eve, Satan "sought to destroy the world," not knowing "the mind of God" (Moses 4:6). It may seem odd that one who presumably had retained his memory of the councils in heaven would not know that he could neither destroy the world nor thwart God's plan by enticing Adam and Eve to fall. Perhaps this shows that he had become successful in deceiving even himself. His promise to Eve that she would not die from eating the fruit was a lie, but even more so was the suggestion that God did not want Adam and Eve to eat the fruit because he did not want them to become "as gods, knowing good and evil" (Moses 4:11; see also v. 10). Eve ate the fruit because it was "good for food," "pleasant to the eyes," and—probably most important—would "make her wise." She gave some to Adam, and he ate also (Moses 4:12).

God responded to the eating of the fruit by addressing each of the participants individually. Satan was told that although he could harm Eve's posterity, Eve's posterity would do him greater harm. The singular pronoun in the text suggests Christ, whose conquest of sin and death through the Atonement would neutralize Satan and his works (Moses 4:21; cf. Heb. 2:14). God's sober words to Eve and Adam are sometimes mistaken for curses. Rather, they are explanations of the conditions they had brought upon themselves; they were introductions to what life would be like on fallen earth. Eve was told that childbearing would be difficult, that her desire would be to her husband, and that he would rule over her (see Moses 4:22). The second of these is not explained in the scriptures but has its corollary in the natural desire of Adam for his wife that was announced when Eve was first created (see Moses 3:24). President Kimball and other Church leaders stated the obvious preference for *preside* rather than *rule* as part of the relationship between the man and the woman.[2] Adam's introduction to mortality focuses on one thing: life would be difficult. In the earth's fallen condition, the ground would be "cursed," and it would take hard work and sorrow to make a living from it. The earth would naturally bring forth "thorns" and "thistles" rather than edible food, which could only be produced through daily toil and perspiration. Finally, we would work hard all our lives, and then we would die (Moses 4:23–24; see also v. 25).

In our day Church leaders have placed special emphasis on the need for us to fulfill righteously the responsibilities that were first given to Adam and Eve: "By divine design, fathers are to preside over their families in love and righteousness and are responsible to provide the necessities of life and protection for their families. Mothers are primarily responsible for the nurture of their children. In these sacred responsibilities, fathers and mothers are obligated to help one another as equal partners."[3]

After the Fall the process of mortal life commenced as the Lord told Adam and Eve it would. They labored to make a living from the ground and in due time brought forth children, and their children in turn had children. Adam and Eve were not left without revelation, for the Lord gave them commandments by his own voice. When they were obedient to what they had been told, an angel taught them more, as did the Holy Ghost (see Moses 5:1–9). God revealed to them the first principles and ordinances of the gospel and explained the plan of salvation (see Moses 6:50–63; D&C 29:42). Adam was "caught away by the Spirit of the Lord, and was carried down into the water, and was laid under the water, and was brought forth out of the water. And thus he was baptized, and the Spirit of God descended upon him, and thus he was born of the Spirit, and became quickened in the inner man" (Moses 6:64–65).

At some point following their expulsion from Eden, Adam and Eve were able to look back on their experiences and rejoice that they had entered into the fallen world. Adam said (Moses 5:10):

> Blessed be the name of God, for because of my transgression
> [a] my eyes are opened,
> [b] and in this life I shall have joy,
> [c] and again in the flesh I shall see God.

Eve responded (Moses 5:11):

> Were it not for our transgression
> [a] we never should have had seed,
> [b] and never should have known good and evil,
> [c] [and never should have known] the joy of our redemption,
> and the eternal life which God giveth unto all the obedient.

It is clear that in this later retrospect Adam and Eve were able to see that the Fall was a good thing, a positive step forward in the progression of God's children. From these passages and others, we can summarize the following about their circumstances in the Garden before their transgression:

1. *There was no death.* The scriptures teach that Adam and Eve introduced death into the world. Prior to their fall, they and all other living things on earth were immortal (Moses 3:17; 4:8–9, 25; 6:48; 2 Ne. 2:22).

2. *Adam and Eve could not have children.* The scriptures do not tell us why Adam and Eve could not have children before the Fall. That their eyes were not yet opened and they did not know they were naked may not have been the only factors (Moses 5:11; 6:48; 2 Ne. 2:23, 25).

3. *Adam and Eve were in the presence of God.* While they were in Eden, our first parents were able to interact with God in person. The earth was a holy and pure place that was suitable for his divine presence. Adam "talked with him and walked with him."[4]

4. Adam and Eve were innocent and did not have a knowledge of good and evil. This situation is difficult for us to understand because it is so different from our own circumstances (see Moses 4:12–13, 28; 5:10–11; Alma 42:3). Adam and Eve were intelligent and otherwise mature persons who were apparently more like young children than like adults with regard to knowing the difference between right and wrong. Yet they had the capacity to choose, and they had a choice between two different courses of action. One course—refraining from eating the fruit—would allow them to stay in Eden. The other—eating the fruit—would cause them to leave. Adam and Eve, like children too young to be baptized, were not morally accountable and thus could not sin. Yet they still had to face the consequences of their actions, just as a child too young to sin cannot escape the natural effects of touching a hot object or falling from a tree.

The scriptures do not present the decision of Adam and Eve as a carefully reasoned choice or as one based on a desire to do the right thing. It is depicted instead as an act of disobedience to God's express wishes (see Gen. 2:17; Rom. 5:17–19; Alma 42:12; D&C 29:40–41; Moses 4:17, 23). Yet we have only a brief narrative, we do not know to what extent the account is figurative, and we do not know how much Adam and Eve understood of the principles involved. In any case our first parents made the right decision, a decision that was in harmony with God's plan, that was absolutely necessary for our continued progress, and that blesses us to the present time. Joseph Smith said: "Adam did not commit sin in eating the fruits, for God had decreed that he should eat and fall. But in compliance with the decree, he should die. Only [that] he should die was the saying of the Lord; therefore the Lord appointed us to fall and also redeemed us."[5]

But why did God not simply create the world in such a

condition that the plan would be underway from the beginning? Why did God place Adam and Eve in a paradise with the anticipation that it and they would need to fall? I suggest a twofold answer. First, all things were created to be *very good,* because that is the nature of God and his work. God creates things that are *organized, spiritual,* and in harmony with his order. Second, perhaps man needed to exercise his own agency to fall and die because God would not force those conditions on us. According to Alma, our fallen condition is something we brought on ourselves (see Alma 42:12). Yet if God would not impose the conditions of mortality on us, then it is reasonable to suggest that Adam and Eve, who made decisions that affect every human being, were not acting without our specific approval. Because they were representing us in what they did, it makes sense that in the premortal councils we sustained them to act in our behalf.

THE PLAN OF SALVATION

Joseph Smith taught: "After God had created the heavens and the earth, he came down and on the sixth day said, 'Let us make man in our own image.' In whose image? In the image of Gods created they them, male and female: innocent, harmless, and spotless, bearing the same character and the same image as the Gods. And when man fell he did not lose his image but his character, still retaining the image of his maker."[6] After the Fall our first parents were in a condition that differed substantially from that of the Garden of Eden. We can summarize their circumstances, and those of their descendants to the present day, as follows:

1. All living things are mortal. Physical death would become the unavoidable fate not only of Adam and Eve but of all life that would exist on earth (1 Cor. 15:22; Moses 3:17; 4:8–9, 25; 6:48; 2 Ne. 2:22; Alma 42:6). The Fall put into operation the laws of nature as we know them and made all life subject to a process of aging, death, and decay.

2. *Adam and Eve were capable of having posterity.* This doctrine, unique to Latter-day Saints, is found in the teachings of Eve, Enoch, and Lehi (Moses 5:11; 6:48; 2 Ne. 2:23, 25). The Fall made it possible for us to come to earth, and it presumably began the process of reproduction for plants and animals as well.

3. *Adam and Eve were banished from God's presence and thereby suffered spiritual death.* In coming to earth, we leave God and enter an unholy, fallen world that cannot endure God's presence. We inherit a fallen nature that makes us unclean, and our own sins make us unworthy of Heavenly Father. All humans are "conceived in sin," meaning that they are born into a world of sin. And "when they begin to grow up, sin conceiveth in their hearts" (Moses 6:55). Thus they become "carnal, sensual, and devilish, by nature" (Alma 42:10). Our resulting alienation from God is spiritual death (see Alma 42:6–11, 14; Hel. 14:16; D&C 29:40–41; 67:11–12).

4. *Adam and Eve were no longer innocent but had a knowledge of good and evil.* In obtaining this knowledge, their eyes were opened, they became morally accountable, and they could sin (Moses 4:12–13, 28; 5:10–11; Alma 42:3).

Of these consequences of the Fall, the capacity to bring forth children and the capacity to discern good from evil are profound blessings and sources of joy. Although being able to know right from wrong and being accountable for our choices creates the potential for danger, error, and sorrow, we cannot progress under any other circumstances. But the remaining consequences of the Fall are another matter. The scriptures do not describe physical and spiritual death as blessings but as monsters—enemies so powerful that we cannot withstand them (see 2 Ne. 9:10, 26).

Physical death was conquered once and for all through the atonement of Jesus Christ. "As in Adam all die, even so in Christ shall all be made alive" (1 Cor. 15:22). This is an automatic gift of the Atonement that will come to all people and does not require any act on our part. "This is wherein all men are redeemed, because the death of Christ bringeth to pass the resurrection, which bringeth to pass a redemption from an endless sleep, from which sleep all men shall be awakened by the power of God when the trump shall sound; . . . being redeemed and loosed from this eternal band of death, which death is a temporal death" (Morm. 9:13; cf. Alma 11:41–44).

Spiritual death—a consequence of the Fall and of our own sins—can also only be remedied through the atonement of Jesus Christ. Our sins keep us from the presence of our Heavenly Father and place us in a state of separation, alienation, and estrangement from him. Amulek taught that God "shall not save his people in their sins. . . . For . . . he hath said that no unclean thing can inherit the kingdom of heaven; therefore, how can ye be saved, except ye inherit the kingdom of heaven? Therefore, ye cannot be saved in your sins" (Alma 11:36–37; cf. 1 Ne. 10:21). Amulek taught further, "For it is expedient that an atonement should be made; for according to the great plan of the Eternal God there must be an atonement made, or else all mankind must unavoidably perish; yea, all are hardened; yea, all are fallen and are lost, and must perish except it be through the atonement which it is expedient should be made" (Alma 34:9). Alma added: "And now, there was no means to reclaim men from this fallen state. . . . Therefore, according to justice, the plan of redemption could not be brought about, only on conditions of repentance of men in this probationary state. . . . And thus we see that all mankind were fallen, and they were in the grasp of justice; yea, the justice of God, which consigned them forever to be cut off from his presence" (Alma 42:12–14).

Spiritual death, as the scriptures teach, places us in a situation from which we cannot save ourselves. The gap between us and our Heavenly Father is bridged by Jesus Christ, who takes our sins from us and pays their penalty when we repent and exercise faith in him. Through his atonement we are made sinless before the law and thus worthy to enter the presence of God. But because it is *Jesus'* worthiness and not our own that makes us clean, we will always be in his debt and always view him as our Savior. Alma taught, "And now, the plan of mercy could not be brought about except an atonement should be made; therefore God himself atoneth for the sins of the world, to bring about the plan of mercy, to appease the demands of justice, that God might be a perfect, just God, and a merciful God also" (Alma 42:15). Amulek summarized, "He shall come into the world to redeem his people; and he shall take upon him the transgressions of those who believe on his name; and these are they that shall have eternal life" (Alma 11:40).

As Joseph Smith said, because of the Fall, we have lost the divine nature we possessed in the Garden of Eden. But "through the atonement of Christ and the resurrection and obedience in the gospel, we shall again be conformed to the image of his Son Jesus Christ. Then we shall have attained to the image, glory, and character of God."[7] Because Christ redeems us from sin and death, we too can rejoice, as did Adam and Eve, that we are here in this testing ground of mortality. The gospel—the good news of salvation—is Christ's invitation to us to accept the gift of his atoning sacrifice and to allow his grace and mercy to guide us back to our Father in Heaven. Jesus said, "Listen to him who is the advocate with the Father, who is pleading your cause before him—Saying: Father, behold the sufferings and death of him who did no sin, in whom thou wast well pleased; behold the blood of thy Son which was shed, the blood of him whom thou gavest that thyself might be glorified; wherefore, Father, spare these my brethren that believe on my name, that they may come unto me and have everlasting life" (D&C 45:3–5).

Notes

1. See the discussion in chapter 6 of this book.

2. E.g., Spencer W. Kimball, "The Blessings and Responsibilities of Womanhood," *Ensign,* March 1976, 72.

3. "The Family: A Proclamation to the World," *Ensign,* November 1995, 102.

4. Andrew F. Ehat and Lyndon W. Cook, eds., *The Words of Joseph Smith: The Contemporary Accounts of the Nauvoo Discourses of the Prophet Joseph* (Provo, Utah: Religious Studies Center, Brigham Young University, 1980), 344; spelling standardized.

5. Ibid., 63; spelling, capitalization, and punctuation standardized.

6. Ibid., 231; capitalization and punctuation standardized.

7. Ibid.; capitalization and punctuation standardized.

9

FROM ADAM TO ENOCH

THE EARLIEST GENERATIONS AFTER the days of Adam and Eve constitute perhaps the most mysterious time in scriptural history. From the standard works, we know it was an amazing age of great things in which the conflicting kingdoms of God and Satan were present and in which the power and appeal of each could be seen. The Bible devotes only a few verses to the period from the death of Adam to the translation of the city of Enoch. But the Restoration contributes much more. The Joseph Smith Translation account in the book of Moses adds significant new information, particularly concerning the generation of Enoch.

Though our scriptural information for this period is sketchy, we are nonetheless able to gain an overview of the people and events that made this early time an important era. From what we know of it, we can see that a most characteristic feature was contrast—the ever-present contrast between the works of God and Satan. The scriptures contain two parallel histories, one of Satan's kingdom and another of God's. God's way of living leads to happiness, the establishment of Zion, and

100

sanctification. Satan's way of living leads to sorrow, curses, and destruction.

THE WORKS OF SATAN

In each dispensation in which the Lord has established his work, the adversary has established his own as well. Satan's counterfeit kingdom has been successful in creating sorrow and suffering, while the Lord's has led faithful individuals into happiness and eternal glory. Perhaps not long after the children of Adam and Eve grew to maturity, the adversary began to sow the seeds of sin and disbelief among many of them. The scriptures record that after Adam and Eve taught their children the gospel, Satan came among them and "commanded them, saying: Believe it not; and they believed it not, and they loved Satan more than God. And men began from that time forth to be carnal, sensual, and devilish" (Moses 5:13).

The scriptures give us the story of Cain as a model of apostasy and as an example of the nature of humans when they yield themselves to the influence of evil. Modern revelation provides significant information not contained in the Bible. Cain rejected God's way (see Moses 5:25–26) and loved and made a covenant with Satan (see Moses 5:28–31). As a result of his crime, God cursed him that the ground would not bear for him (see Moses 5:36–37) and cast him out of his presence (see Moses 5:39, 41).

But this was not an isolated incident in history: "And thus the works of darkness began to prevail among all the sons of men" (Moses 5:55). "And in those days Satan had great dominion among men, and raged in their hearts; and from thenceforth came wars and bloodshed; and a man's hand was against his own brother, in administering death, because of secret works, seeking for power" (Moses 6:15).

Multiplied over many years and many lives, the process continued: "Since the day that I created them, have they gone astray, and have denied me, and have sought their own counsels in the dark; and in their own abominations have they devised murder, and have not kept the commandments, which I gave unto their father, Adam. Wherefore, they have foresworn themselves, and, by their oaths, they have brought upon themselves death" (Moses 6:28–29).

This level of evil continued into the days of Enoch, who saw a vision of Satan and his works in which dramatic symbols put in vivid focus the adversary's desires and objectives. "And he beheld Satan; and he had a great chain in his hand, and it veiled the whole face of the earth with darkness; and he looked up and laughed, and his angels rejoiced" (Moses 7:26). And "the Lord said unto Enoch: Behold these thy brethren; they are the workmanship of mine own hands, and I gave unto them their knowledge, in the day I created them; and in the Garden of Eden, gave I unto man his agency; and unto thy brethren have I said, and also given commandment, that they should love one another, and that they should choose me, their Father; but behold, they are without affection, and they hate their own blood" (Moses 7:32–33).

By the time of Noah, humankind had become so wicked that the following unprecedented words are recorded: "And God saw that the wickedness of men had become great in the earth; and every man was lifted up in the imagination of the thoughts of his heart, being only evil continually" (Moses 8:22). That generation was found to be so wicked that its people were not allowed to pollute the earth any longer by their presence on it. The Lord decreed that all living things on earth would be destroyed by flood, with the exception of those who would be spared so God could begin anew his creative work and reestablish his covenant among men. As it will be at the end of the world, evil must be eliminated, whether it be through repentance or through destruction. For almost all people in Noah's day, the option taken was destruction at the hand of the Lord.

THE TRIUMPH OF ZION

While it is clear from the scriptures that the world as a whole in those ancient days could be characterized as extremely evil, still the records tell us that at the same time there were people who were extremely righteous. The same generations that produced humanity at its lowest level also produced men and women whose disposition to obey and serve God is unparalleled in human history. Enoch's society was found worthy to be taken as a group from the earth to escape its corruptions and enjoy the blessings of a higher sphere. Later, the community of Melchizedek followed.

Genesis 5 lists the genealogies of the lineage through whom the priesthood and the covenants of the gospel continued, beginning with Adam and ending with the sons of Noah. Little is given aside from the genealogical information. One can imagine that great things were manifested in the lives of righteous Saints. Concerning the ministry of the great patriarch Enoch, the biblical account states only the following: "And Enoch walked with God: and he was not; for God took him" (Gen. 5:24).

In the summer of 1830, when the Prophet Joseph Smith began his work on his New Translation of the Bible, he probably knew little about Zion and almost nothing about Enoch.

But among the foremost contributions of the Joseph Smith Translation is the addition of several pages of entirely new material dealing with Enoch's period and his labors to create Zion among his people. The book of Moses tells us that in spite of the widespread wickedness of those days, the work of the Lord was continuing: "And thus the Gospel began to be preached, from the beginning, being declared by holy angels sent forth from the presence of God, and by his own voice, and by the gift of the Holy Ghost" (Moses 5:58). Moses 6 and 8 supplement the genealogies of the patriarchs by adding information concerning them that is not found in the corresponding narrative in Genesis 5. The most substantial contribution of this section, however, is the large amount of material concerning the great prophet Enoch and his people. Whereas Genesis discusses Enoch in only six brief verses (see Gen. 5:18–19, 21–24), the Joseph Smith Translation account in Moses 6 and 7 discusses his life, mission, and revelations in 116 verses (see Moses 6:21, 25–8:2).

The biographical material revealed to Joseph Smith has no counterpart in the Bible. Like Joseph Smith and many other prophets, Enoch was called out of obscurity (see Moses 6:26–31). The Lord told him, "Open thy mouth, and it shall be filled, and I will give thee utterance. . . . Behold my Spirit is upon you, wherefore all thy words will I justify" (Moses 6:32, 34). The Lord said, "Anoint thine eyes with clay, and wash them, and thou shalt see" (Moses 6:35). When Enoch did as he was commanded, "he beheld the spirits that God had created; and he beheld also things which were not visible to the natural eye; and from thenceforth came the saying abroad in the land: A seer hath the Lord raised up unto his people" (Moses 6:36). As one who could see things "not visible to the natural eye," Enoch is a prototypical seer—a *see-er,* one who really sees. Enoch's tremendous spiritual gifts were apparent to the righteous and the wicked alike: "All men were offended because of him" (Moses 6:37). They said, "There is a strange thing in the land; a wild man hath come among us. And it came to pass when they heard him, no man laid hands on him; for fear came on all them that heard him; for he walked with God" (Moses 6:38–39). "And as Enoch spake forth the words of God, the people trembled, and could not stand in his presence" (Moses 6:47).

In an 1835 revelation to Joseph Smith, we learn that "Enoch was twenty-five years old when he was ordained under the hand of Adam; and he was sixty-five and Adam blessed him" (D&C 107:48). Three years before Adam's death, Enoch was present with Adam and his righteous descendants at a great meeting at the valley of Adam-ondi-Ahman, where Adam "bestowed upon them his last blessing" (D&C 107:53). These and other biographical details "were all written in the book of Enoch, and are to be testified of in due time" (D&C 107:57).[1]

Enoch led his people in the ways of God and established among them Zion—"THE PURE IN HEART" (D&C 97:21). While the wicked of Enoch's generation were cursed, "the Lord came and dwelt with his people, and they dwelt in righteousness" (Moses 7:16). "The fear of the Lord was upon all nations, so great was the glory of the Lord, which was upon his people. And the Lord blessed the land, and they were blessed upon the mountains, and upon the high places, and did flourish. And the Lord called his people ZION, because they were of one heart and one mind, and dwelt in righteousness; and there was no poor among them. And Enoch continued his preaching in righteousness unto the people of God. And it came to pass in his days, that he built a city that was called the City of Holiness, even ZION. And it came to pass that Enoch talked with the

Lord; and he said unto the Lord: Surely Zion shall dwell in safety forever. But the Lord said unto Enoch: Zion have I blessed, but the residue of the people have I cursed" (Moses 7:17–20). Enoch "saw the Lord, and he walked with him, and was before his face continually; and he walked with God three hundred and sixty-five years, making him four hundred and thirty years old when he was translated" (D&C 107:49).

While the rest of the world stayed on the course that would lead eventually to destruction by the Flood, "Zion, in process of time, was taken up into heaven. And the Lord said unto Enoch: Behold mine abode forever" (Moses 7:21). Joseph Smith taught, "He selected Enoch, whom he directed, and gave his law unto [him] and to the people who were with him; and when the world in general would not obey the commands of God, after walking with God, he translated Enoch and his church, and the priesthood or government of heaven, was taken away."[2] "And all the days of Zion, in the days of Enoch, were three hundred and sixty-five years. And Enoch and all his people walked with God, and he dwelt in the midst of Zion; and it came to pass that Zion was not, for God received it up into his own bosom; and from thence went forth the saying, Zion is Fled" (Moses 7:68–69; cf. D&C 38:4).

Joseph Smith taught that Enoch and his people were not exalted then but were translated and appointed to minister to others:

"Now this Enoch, God reserved unto himself that he should not die at that time and appointed unto him a ministry unto terrestrial bodies, of whom there has been but little revealed. . . . He is a ministering angel, to minister to those who shall be heirs of salvation. . . . Now the doctrine of translation is a power which belongs to this priesthood. There are many things which belong to the powers of the priesthood and the keys thereof that have been kept hid from before the foundation of the world. They are hid from the wise and prudent to be revealed in the last times. Many may have supposed that the doctrine of translation was a doctrine whereby men were taken immediately into the presence of God and into an eternal fulness. But this is a mistaken idea. Their place of habitation is that of the terrestrial order and a place prepared for such characters he held in reserve to be ministering angels unto many planets, and who as yet have not entered into so great a fulness as those who are resurrected from the dead."[3]

After the translation of Enoch's people, many others were taken to join them: "They were caught up by the powers of heaven into Zion" (Moses 7:27). By the time of Noah, perhaps the only options were translation or destruction in the Flood. But even after the Flood, the entire community of Melchizedek was translated and joined the city of Enoch.[4]

Zion in the Last Days

The sanctification of the community of Enoch has provided the pattern for all other righteous societies to follow. Beginning not long after the Enoch material was revealed in the winter of 1830–31, additional revelations came to Joseph Smith that taught him how to begin the process of building Zion in the latter-day Church. Coming as these revelations did early in the Restoration, they have helped plot the course for the Saints of the latter days, who under the direction of modern prophets strive to build Zion in accordance with the Lord's will. We should not be surprised that Joseph Smith prophesied that in our own quest to build Zion, we too will be successful, just as Enoch and his people were:

"The building up of Zion is a cause that has interested the

people of God in every age. It is a theme upon which prophets, priests, and kings have dwelt with peculiar delight. They have looked forward with joyful anticipation to the day in which we live, and fired with heavenly and joyful anticipations they have sung, and written, and prophesied of this our day. But they died without the sight. We are the favored people that God has made choice of to bring about the latter-day glory. It is left for us to see, participate in, and help to roll forward the latter-day glory, 'the dispensation of the fulness of times,' when God will 'gather together all things that are in heaven, and all things that are upon the earth, even in one' [Eph. 1:10], when the Saints of God will be gathered in one from every nation, and kindred, and people, and tongue, when the Jews will be gathered together into one, [and] the wicked will also be gathered together to be destroyed, as spoken of by the prophets. The spirit of God will also dwell with his people and be withdrawn from the rest of the nations. And all things, whether in heaven or on earth, will be in one, even in Christ.

"The heavenly priesthood will unite with the earthly to bring about those great purposes. And whilst we are thus united in the one common cause to roll forth the kingdom of God, the heavenly priesthood are not idle spectators. The spirit of God will be showered down from above; it will dwell in our midst. The blessings of the Most High will rest upon our tabernacles, and our name will be handed down to future ages. Our children will rise up and call us blessed, and generations yet unborn will dwell with peculiar delight upon the scenes that we have passed through, the privations that we have endured, the untiring zeal that we have manifested, the insurmountable difficulties that we have overcome in laying the foundation of a work that brought about the glory and blessings which they will realize, a work that God and angels have contemplated with delight for generations past, that fired the souls of the ancient patriarchs and prophets, a work that is destined to bring about the destruction of the powers of darkness, the renovation of the earth, the glory of God, and the salvation of the human family."[5]

As part of "the renovation of the earth," Enoch and his people will return to labor with us for "the salvation of the human family." "And righteousness will I send down out of heaven; and truth will I send forth out of the earth, to bear testimony of mine Only Begotten; . . . and righteousness and truth will I cause to sweep the earth as with a flood, to gather out mine elect from the four quarters of the earth, unto a place which I shall prepare, an Holy City" (Moses 7:62). Joseph Smith asked, "Now I ask how righteousness and truth are going to sweep the earth as with a flood. I will answer: Men and angels are to be co-workers in bringing to pass this great work, and a Zion is to be prepared—even a New Jerusalem—for the elect that are to be gathered from the four quarters of the earth, and to be established an holy city. For the tabernacle of the Lord shall be with them."[6] The Lord said that Enoch's people were "separated from the earth, and were received unto [him]-self—a city reserved until a day of righteousness shall come—a day which was sought for by all holy men" (D&C 45:12). To Enoch he said, "Then shalt thou and all thy city meet them there, and we will receive them into our bosom, and they shall see us; and we will fall upon their necks, and they shall fall upon our necks, and we will kiss each other; and there shall be mine abode, and it shall be Zion, which shall come forth out of all the creations which I have made; and for the space of a thousand years the earth shall rest" (Moses 7:63–64).

In Enoch's day the choice for all people was to join Zion or remain in the world. While the citizens of the kingdom of God established a community of peace on the principles of faith and righteousness, the citizens of Satan's kingdom continued in their unrepentant ways and reaped a harvest of sorrow and destruction. For most of humankind, the history of the world from Adam to Enoch was a continuing chronicle of tragedy. The sad experience of those who chose evil proves that what Alma said is true: "Wickedness never was happiness" (Alma 41:10). We live today in a world saturated with unrighteousness, but it is in this world that our own great work of building Zion is taking place.

NOTES

1. That the Enoch material in the Joseph Smith Translation (Moses 6–7) is not the promised "book of Enoch" is clear from the fact that this statement (D&C 107:57) came four years after the Enoch passages were revealed.

2. *Times and Seasons,* 15 July 1842, 857.

3. Andrew F. Ehat and Lyndon W. Cook, eds., *The Words of Joseph Smith: The Contemporary Accounts of the Nauvoo Discourses of the Prophet Joseph* (Provo, Utah: Religious Studies Center, Brigham Young University, 1980), 41; spelling, capitalization, and punctuation standardized.

4. I.V. Gen. 14:27, 30–34. See also chapter 10 of this volume.

5. *Times and Seasons,* 2 May 1842, 776; capitalization and punctuation standardized.

6. *Messenger and Advocate,* November 1835, 209; capitalization and punctuation standardized.

10

METHUSELAH, NOAH, AND MELCHIZEDEK

THE TRANSLATION OF THE CITY OF ENOCH did not end God's work to build Zion on earth, for, as Joseph Smith taught, "The building up of Zion is a cause that has interested the people of God in *every* age."[1] Though the Flood would delay the creation of other Zion communities until after the waters subsided, Zion on earth was always the objective. We will examine the period from Enoch to Melchizedek in light of modern revelation—primarily the Joseph Smith Translation and the teachings and revelations of the Prophet Joseph Smith.

METHUSELAH

Methuselah, a son of Enoch, is mentioned in only six verses in the Old Testament (see Gen. 5:21–22, 25–27; 1 Chr. 1:3), and those verses tell us very little about his life. A revelation to Joseph Smith provides additional insights. Methuselah was ordained to the priesthood by his forefather Adam (see D&C 107:50), and Methuselah, in turn, ordained his grandson Noah (see D&C 107:52). Methuselah participated in the great meeting at Adam-ondi-Ahman three years before Adam's death at which Adam gave his righteous posterity "his last blessing" (D&C 107:53). Inasmuch as Noah was born after that meeting, Methuselah formed a link between Adam, the father of the human family, and Noah, who would become the new father of the human family following the Flood.[2]

The Joseph Smith Translation adds material regarding Methuselah for which there is no biblical counterpart. In it we learn that when Enoch's city was translated, Methuselah "was not taken, that the covenants of the Lord might be fulfilled, which he made to Enoch" (Moses 8:2). Enoch had learned through revelation that the Flood would destroy the population of the earth. The covenant referred to in this verse was that from his lineage a faithful family would survive to repopulate the planet, and thus all the people thereafter would stem from him (see Moses 7:42, 50–52; JST at Gen. 6:18[3]). Of necessity a family line from Enoch—presumably worthy to be translated—would remain behind. Methuselah prophesied correctly that all the human family would descend from him, but "he took glory unto himself" (Moses 8:3).

NOAH AND THE COVENANT

Noah and his three sons—Japheth, Shem, and Ham—were righteous men. The Joseph Smith Translation tells us that they obeyed the Lord to the degree that they were called "the sons of God" (Moses 8:13). Elsewhere in modern revelation we learn that those who embrace the gospel, who receive the Lord and believe on his name (see D&C 11:30), "are sons and daughters in [God's] kingdom" (D&C 25:1), that those who accept the message of his prophets and look forward to redemption in Christ are "his seed" (Mosiah 15:11), and that in making covenants we become "the children of Christ, his sons, and his daughters" (Mosiah 5:7). Noah and his sons were such men. Moreover, the Joseph Smith Translation tells us that they "walked with God" (Moses 8:27), a phrase used elsewhere with regard to Enoch and his people in Zion before their translation (see Moses 7:69).

Noah received the priesthood from his grandfather Methuselah when he was ten years old (see D&C 107:52), but "the Lord ordained Noah after his own order"—perhaps with reference to his specific calling to "declare his Gospel unto the children of men, even as it was given unto Enoch" (Moses 8:19). Noah "taught the things of God" (Moses 8:16), including faith, repentance, baptism, and the reception of the Holy Ghost (see Moses 8:24). In short, the gospel of Jesus Christ was the message, as it has been whenever the gospel has been found on the earth in its fulness. Regarding this Joseph Smith taught, "Now taking it for granted that the scriptures say what they mean and mean what they say, we have sufficient grounds to go on and prove from the Bible that the gospel has always been the same, the ordinances to fulfill its requirements the same, and the officers to officiate the same, and the signs and fruits resulting from the promises the same."[4]

The Latter-day Saint view that ancient righteous people had the gospel is not shared by other Christians. But how else could it be? If God spoke with worthy men like Noah, and if accepting the gospel of Christ is the only means of salvation, as the Bible teaches (see John 3:16, 36; 1 John 5:11–12), then why would God deny its blessings to honorable men and women who lived before Jesus? These considerations should cause all Christians to conclude, as Joseph Smith did, that "much instruction has been given to man since the beginning which we have not."[5]

We are certainly blessed by the restored scriptures that teach us of believers in Christ from earlier days.[6]

Because the gospel was always the same as it is now, we can draw certain conclusions about Noah, as did the Prophet Joseph Smith: "As Noah was a preacher of righteousness he must have been baptized and ordained to the priesthood by the laying on of the hands, and so forth."[7] Indeed, God "continued to [Noah] the keys, the covenants, the power, and the glory with which he blessed Adam at the beginning."[8] Noah warned the people that rejection of his message would bring destruction: "If men do not repent, [the Lord] will send in the floods upon them" (Moses 8:17). Accordingly, "Noah called upon the children of men that they should repent; but they hearkened not unto his words" (Moses 8:20). And after calling upon them to observe the first principles and ordinances of the gospel, he said, "And if ye do not this, the floods will come in upon you." Even so, "they hearkened not" (Moses 8:24). These passages, unique to the Joseph Smith Translation, place the ensuing Flood in a context that is not found in the Bible. The Lord through his servant Noah (and undoubtedly through others before him) gave the people of the world every warning and every opportunity to change before leaving them to their destruction.

The Joseph Smith Translation makes several references to a covenant God made with Enoch and later renewed with Noah. From the evidence preserved in the text, it appears that this covenant had the following three parts:

1. *The entire human family will descend from Enoch and Noah.* We have already seen this promise in the account concerning Enoch's son (and Noah's grandfather) Methuselah (see Moses 8:2–3). The Lord told Noah, "With thee will I establish my

covenant, even as I have sworn unto thy father, Enoch, that of thy posterity shall come all nations" (JST at Gen. 6:18[9]).

2. *The inhabitants of the earth will never again be destroyed by flood.* The Joseph Smith Translation teaches that this promise was made earlier to Enoch (see Moses 7:50–51; JST at Gen. 9:9, 12[10]), but it provides an interesting context—not found in the Bible—for the renewal of the blessing to Noah. The Joseph Smith Translation change at Genesis 8:21 shows that the promise came as the result of Noah's request to the Lord in behalf of the living things of the earth. Noah said, "I will call on the name of the Lord, that he will not again curse the ground any more for man's sake, . . . and that he will not again smite any more every thing living, as he hath done."[11] The Lord honored Noah's request and promised that he would never again send a flood to destroy all the humans and animals (see JST at Gen. 9:9–15[12]). Noah served as an intercessor in behalf of his descendants and the rest of life on earth, as is shown in several changes in the Joseph Smith Translation (see JST at Gen. 9:9, 12, 15, 17[13]). Just as Adam at the beginning of human history was God's representative and vice-regent on earth, so Noah, the new Adam, made covenants with God in behalf of his children and all other life.

This promise came with a sign. The rainbow, which even now often shows that a rainstorm is ending, would signify that God would never again destroy the world by flood (see Gen. 9:12–15[14]). Concerning the destruction of the world that will take place in the last days, Joseph Smith taught: "I have asked of the Lord concerning his coming, and while asking, the Lord gave me a sign and said: 'In the days of Noah I set a bow in the heavens as a sign and token that in any year that the bow should be seen, the Lord would not come; but there should be seed time [and] harvest during that year. But whenever you see the bow withdraw, it shall be a token that there shall be famine, pestilence, and great distress among the nations.'"[15]

3. *Zion, the City of Enoch, will return to earth.* In a dramatic departure from the biblical text at Genesis 9:16, the Joseph Smith Translation account reveals new and significant information concerning the people of Enoch.

King James Translation	*Joseph Smith Translation*
And the bow shall be in the cloud; and I will look upon it, that I may remember the everlasting covenant	And the bow shall be in the cloud; and I will look upon it, that I may remember the everlasting covenant, which I made unto thy father Enoch; that, when men should keep all my commandments, Zion should again come on the Earth, the city of Enoch which I have caught up unto myself. And this is mine everlasting covenant that I establish with you,[16] that when thy posterity shall embrace the truth, and look upward, then shall Zion look downward, and all the heavens shall shake with gladness, and the earth shall tremble with joy; and the general assembly of the church of the first-born shall come down out of heaven, and possess the earth, and shall have place until the end come. And this is mine everlasting covenant, which I made with thy father Enoch. And the bow shall be in the cloud, and I will establish my covenant unto thee, which I have
between God and every living creature of all flesh that is upon the earth.	made between me and thee, for every living creature of all flesh that shall be upon the earth.
	(I.V. Gen. 9:21–24)

In addition to being a sign that God will no longer destroy the world by flood, the rainbow is a sign of the return of the city of Enoch. This is unique restored doctrine not appreciated (or known) by most Latter-day Saints. When we see a rainbow in the sky, we should see it as a sign that Zion will return. It will return when people on earth will keep God's commandments, when Noah's posterity will "embrace the truth, and look upward" (JST Gen. 9:22). The context is millennial, and Enoch's city cannot return until its counterpart, the latter-day Zion on earth, is established and ready to receive it. Elsewhere in the Joseph Smith Translation we read: "Righteousness and truth will I cause to sweep the earth as with a flood, to gather out mine elect from the four quarters of the earth, unto a place which I shall prepare, an Holy City, that my people may gird up their loins, and be looking forth for the time of my coming; for there shall be my tabernacle, and it shall be called Zion, a New Jerusalem. And the Lord said unto Enoch: Then shalt thou and all thy city meet them there, and we will receive them into our bosom, and they shall see us; and we will fall upon their necks, and they shall fall upon our necks, and we will kiss each other; and there shall be mine abode, and it shall be Zion, which shall come forth out of all the creations which I have made; and for the space of a thousand years the earth shall rest" (Moses 7:62–64).

The general assembly of the church of the first-born will come down to earth from heaven. These are persons who have been sealed up to eternal life, such as the inhabitants of the City of Enoch and others who were translated anciently. They also include those who will be with Jesus at his coming— faithful Saints who will be resurrected at his coming and who will return to earth with him (see D&C 88:96–98).

Even long after the translation of the City of Enoch, that

community served as a model and a goal. The record preserves occasions when faithful Saints after Noah looked to it as the embodiment of their own aspirations (see I.V. Gen. 13:13; 14:27–34). Early in the latter-day restoration, the Lord revealed the story of Enoch and his city so we can similarly lift our sights with a vision of how to build Zion in our own time (see D&C 38:4; 45:12–14; 76:57, 67).

Noah was a great man, chosen to preach the gospel of repentance, to preserve a faithful family through the Flood, to lead God's people in his generation, and to father all the human race that would come after him. Yet there is more to Noah's significance than can be gleaned from the scriptures. Joseph Smith taught, "Christ is the great High Priest, Adam next."[17] And, "The priesthood was first given to Adam . . . then to Noah, who is Gabriel; he stands next in authority to Adam in the priesthood. He was called of God to this office and was the father of all living in his day, and to him was given the dominion."[18] Hence, the hierarchy of God's priesthood holders in the human family begins with Christ, then Adam, and then Noah—making Noah third in rank among all the bearers of the holy priesthood. Moreover, Noah was Gabriel. How fitting that this great man would have the assignment to return to earth as a spirit messenger (see D&C 129:1, 3; 130:5) to prepare selected participants for the coming of the Savior in the flesh (see Luke 1:11–20, 26–38; and probably Matt. 1:20–24; 2:13, 19–20; and possibly Luke 2:8–14).[19]

MELCHIZEDEK

Melchizedek is an enigmatic figure in the Old Testament. In Genesis his name appears only one time (see Gen. 14:18), and there he plays but a very minor role in the history of

Abraham. Yet he is mentioned both in Psalms (see 110:4) and in the New Testament (see Heb. 5:6, 10; 6:20; 7:1–28), and there is a discussion of him in the Book of Mormon (see Alma 13:14–19). These references show that much was known of him in antiquity that has not survived in our Bible.[20] The Joseph Smith Translation of Genesis restores remarkable information concerning Melchizedek in a brief overview of his ministry.

Melchizedek's name, like that of most others from ancient Semitic-speaking peoples, can be translated as a sentence and gives praises to his God. The first part, *Melchi-* (Hebrew *malkî*), means "My King" and has reference to God. *Zedek* (Hebrew *ṣedek*) means "righteousness." The name means "My (Divine) King Is Righteousness." The Bible tells us that when Abraham returned from a battle to rescue his nephew Lot from capture, he encountered Melchizedek, the king of Salem. At their meeting, Melchizedek "brought forth bread and wine." The Bible suggests only incidentally a connection between the bread and wine and the fact that Melchizedek "was the priest of the most high God" (Gen. 14:18). A change in the Joseph Smith Translation speaks volumes: Melchizedek "brought forth bread and wine; and he break bread and blest it; and he blest the wine, he being the priest of the most high God."[21] The bread and wine were thus obviously not a meal but an ordinance conducted by virtue of the priesthood. This was certainly the sacrament, which commemorates (in this case in advance) the atoning flesh and blood of Christ, and this passage is the earliest reference to the sacrament in the scriptures.[22]

Aside from Abraham and his family members, Melchizedek is the only other mortal mentioned in this part of the Bible who worshiped the true God. But as we learn from the Joseph Smith Translation and the Book of Mormon, there were many others. Melchizedek blessed Abraham, and Abraham gave him tithes (see JST at Gen. 14:18–20[23]). As great as Father Abraham was, to whom the Bible dedicates thirteen chapters, our text leads to the conclusion that Melchizedek was the presiding authority, again suggesting that there is much about this period we do not know.

At the conclusion of the account of Melchizedek's meeting with Abraham, at Genesis 14:24, the Joseph Smith Translation adds more than 450 new words that summarize Melchizedek's career.[24] The following excerpts show some of this significant information revealed through the Prophet Joseph Smith:

> Now Melchizedek was a man of faith, who wrought righteousness; and when a child he feared God, and stopped the mouths of lions, and quenched the violence of fire.
>
> He was ordained an high priest after the order of the covenant which God made with Enoch, it being after the order of the Son of God.
>
> For God having sworn unto Enoch and unto his seed with an oath by himself; that every one being ordained after this order and calling should have power, by faith,
>
> to break mountains,
>
> to divide the seas,
>
> to dry up waters,
>
> to turn them out of their course;
>
> to put at defiance the armies of nations,
>
> to divide the earth,
>
> to break every band,
>
> to stand in the presence of God;
>
> to do all things according to his will, according to his command,
>
> [and to] subdue principalities and powers.
>
> And men having this faith, coming up unto this order of God, were translated and taken up into heaven.
>
> (I.V. Gen. 14:26–28, 30–32)

This last passage shows that even after the Flood, some faithful Saints were translated, just as others had been translated in earlier generations between the times of Enoch and Noah (see Moses 7:27). Melchizedek was "a priest of this order." As a righteous leader, "he obtained peace in Salem, and was called the Prince of peace." That he and his people were translated and joined the City of Enoch is evident in the passage that follows: "And his people wrought righteousness, and obtained heaven, and sought for the city of Enoch which God had before taken" (*I.V.* Gen. 14:33–34).

We need not wonder, then, why Melchizedek is such a mysterious person in the Bible. Like Enoch's city, Melchizedek's people were taken from the earth, seemingly without a trace, and thus left behind little historical evidence and apparently had no further influence on world events. Had they remained, presumably some of their history would have been preserved in the Bible. Although some Melchizedek traditions persisted in antiquity, it was left to the Restoration to bring back what the Lord has chosen to let us know about Melchizedek and his people.[25] One remarkable aspect of their history is that while Abraham was in Canaan, engaged in the routines of life punctuated by the experiences that are recorded in the Bible, a great Zion community was flourishing and was eventually translated—perhaps in an adjacent land, or perhaps closer by. Like Methuselah earlier (see Moses 8:2), Abraham was to stay behind to become the father of a great nation.

Melchizedek, being both a "great high priest" (D&C 107:2) and a priest-king, serves as a type of Christ, as we learn from the Joseph Smith Translation of Hebrews 7:3: "For this Melchizedek was ordained a priest after the order of the Son of God, which order was without father, without mother, without descent, having neither beginning of days, nor end of life. And all those who are ordained unto this priesthood are made like unto the Son of God, abiding a priest continually."

"And this Melchizedek, having thus established righteousness, was called the king of heaven by his people, or, in other words, the King of peace. . . .

"He blessed Abram, being the high priest, and the keeper of the storehouse of God; him whom God had appointed to receive tithes for the poor. Wherefore, Abram paid unto him tithes of all that he had, of all the riches which he possessed" (I.V. Gen. 14:36–39).

In addition to the Joseph Smith Translation, modern revelation provides other witnesses for the life and ministry of Melchizedek. The Book of Mormon prophet Alma taught from "the scriptures" (Alma 13:20; see also v. 19) concerning Melchizedek and his people.[26] He spoke of the "many"—the "exceedingly great many"—individuals who had become sanctified on account of their faith, repentance, and good works (Alma 13:12; see also vv. 10–11). He challenged his listeners to become as the people of Melchizedek (see Alma 13:14). In the days of Melchizedek and Abraham, the area of Syria and Canaan constituted not a country but a collection of small city-states ruled by kings. Melchizedek was apparently one such king, ruling a nation that the Book of Mormon describes as "full of all manner of wickedness" (Alma 13:17). But Melchizedek, with faith and priesthood, "did preach repentance unto his people. And behold, they did repent; and Melchizedek did establish peace in the land in his days; therefore he was called the prince of peace" (Alma 13:18). Joseph Smith taught that the name "Salem" for Melchizedek's community has to do not with geography but with the quality of the people who made up its citizenry: "In the original it reads 'king of Shalom,' which signifies king of peace or righteousness."[27] Melchizedek apparently began with the kingdom over which he ruled "under his father" (Alma 13:18). But as his land was transformed into a covenant community of Saints, it is likely that it attracted believers from many separate political entities, just as Enoch's city did and just as the Lord's kingdom does today.

A revelation to Joseph Smith tells us why the higher priesthood bears Melchizedek's name: It is "because Melchizedek was such a great high priest. Before his day it was called *the Holy Priesthood, after the Order of the Son of God*. But out of respect or reverence to the name of the Supreme Being, to avoid the too frequent repetition of his name, they, the church, in ancient days, called that priesthood after Melchizedek" (D&C 107:2–4). Another revelation tells us that Abraham received the priesthood from Melchizedek, "who received it through the lineage of his fathers, even till Noah" (D&C 84:14). Joseph Smith taught that Abraham "received a blessing under the hands of Melchizedek, even the last law, or a fulness of the law or priesthood, which constituted him a king and priest after the order of Melchizedek, or an endless life."[28] This is the blessing of being sealed to exaltation, administered under the hands of one holding the keys of this power. This "was not the power of a prophet, nor apostle, nor patriarch only, but of [a] king and priest to God—to open the windows of heaven and pour out the peace and law of endless life to man."[29] Indeed Melchizedek, whose true kingship was of the kingdom of God, "stood as God to give laws to the people, administering endless lives to the sons and daughters of Adam [by] kingly powers of anointing."[30] It is in this sense that those who will be the heirs of the celestial kingdom "are they who are priests and kings, who have received of his fulness, and of his glory; and are priests of the Most High, after the order of Melchizedek, which was after the order of Enoch, which was after the order of the Only Begotten Son" (D&C 76:56–57).

NOTES

1. *Times and Seasons,* 2 May 1842, 776; emphasis added.

2. This link is a major point of emphasis in the second Lecture on Faith. See *A Compilation Containing the Lectures on Faith,* comp. N. B. Lundwall (Salt Lake City: Bookcraft, n.d.), 18–23.

3. *I.V.* Genesis 8:23. Unless otherwise noted, Joseph Smith Translation references are to the King James Version passage at which the change is made. Chapter and verse numbers are sometimes different in the printed *Inspired Version,* published by the Community of Christ, Independence, Missouri. References preceded by "*I.V.*" are to the chapter and verse numbers as presented in the printed *Inspired Version.* Quoted passages from the Joseph Smith Translation follow the wording in the book of Moses or the *Inspired Version.*

4. *Times and Seasons,* 1 September 1842, 904; spelling and punctuation standardized.

5. *The Evening and the Morning Star,* March 1834, 143.

6. See Kent P. Jackson, *From Apostasy to Restoration* (Salt Lake City: Deseret Book, 1996), 145, 203–4.

7. *Times and Seasons,* 1 September 1842, 904.

8. Andrew F. Ehat and Lyndon W. Cook, eds., *The Words of Joseph Smith: The Contemporary Accounts of the Nauvoo Discourses of the Prophet Joseph* (Provo, Utah: Religious Studies Center, Brigham Young University, 1980), 42; capitalization and punctuation standardized.

9. *I.V.* Genesis 8:23.

10. *I.V.* Genesis 9:15, 18.

11. *I.V.* Genesis 9:6.

12. *I.V.* Genesis 9:15–20.

13. *I.V.* Genesis 9:15, 18, 20, 25. Notice the wording in the following Joseph Smith Translation changes. Genesis 9:9, King James Version: "I establish my covenant with you, *and with* your seed after you," and Joseph Smith Translation: "I will establish my covenant with you, . . . *concerning* your seed after you." Also Genesis 9:15, King James Version: "my

covenant, which is between me and you *and* every living creature," and Joseph Smith Translation: "my covenant, which I have made between me and you, *for* every living creature."

14. See also *I.V.* Genesis 9:15–20.

15. Ehat and Cook, eds., *Words of Joseph Smith,* 332; spelling, capitalization, and punctuation standardized.

16. The *Inspired Version* erroneously omits the clause "that I establish with you," which is on the Joseph Smith Translation manuscript (OT 2, page 31).

17. Ehat and Cook, eds., *Words of Joseph Smith,* 9.

18. Ibid., 8; capitalization and punctuation standardized.

19. We know of Moroni's importance in the Restoration, including his careful tutoring of young Joseph Smith. It seems likely that the same kind of care would be appropriate for those who were to be the earthly guardians and witnesses of Jesus Christ.

20. Two theories regarding Melchizedek deserve notice here. First, based primarily on the phrases "Melchizedek was such a great high priest" (D&C 107:2) and "Shem [son of Noah], the great high priest" (D&C 138:41), some have suggested that Shem and Melchizedek are the same person. But this equation assumes that there can be only one "great high priest," whereas most Latter-day Saints can name others, and the wording in Doctrine and Covenants 107:2 implies that there are more. Also, the reference to Melchizedek's priesthood coming "through the lineage of his fathers, even till Noah" (D&C 84:14) seems to rule out the idea that he is Noah's son.

Second, some have suggested that Melchizedek's Salem was Jerusalem. This belief is based on two lines of reasoning: (a) a linguistic equation of *Rushalimum* and *Urushalim* (Jerusalem's names in the Middle and Late Bronze periods, respectively) with *Yerushalayim* (its name in biblical times), and (b) the use of Salem with reference to Jerusalem in Psalm 76:2. The linguistic equation is complicated and uncertain but possible. The Psalm reference is also not conclusive. In the language of Hebrew poetry, names are used metaphorically to show similarities in characteristics. In disparaging prophecies Jerusalem is called *Sodom* (Isa. 1:10; Rev. 11:8), *Gomorrah* (Isa. 1:10), and *Egypt* (Rev. 11:8). It would not be surprising to see it characterized more positively with a poetic reference to Melchizedek's community.

21. *I.V.* Genesis 14:17.

22. See John Taylor, *Mediation and Atonement* (Salt Lake City: Deseret News, 1882), 83.

23. *I.V.* Genesis 14:18–20.

24. See *I.V.* Genesis 14:25–40.

25. See Ann N. Madsen, "Melchizedek, the Man and the Tradition" (M.A. thesis, Brigham Young University, 1975), 48–111.

26. Presumably from the plates of brass, but possibly from a revelation to one of the Nephite prophets.

27. Ehat and Cook, eds., *Words of Joseph Smith,* 246; spelling, capitalization, and punctuation standardized.

28. Ibid.; spelling and punctuation standardized.

29. Ibid., 245; capitalization and punctuation standardized.

30. Ibid., 244; punctuation standardized.

11

THE COVENANT OF ABRAHAM

G OD'S FRIEND ABRAHAM IS ONE of the pivotal individuals in sacred history. The scriptures record his faith and diligence in serving the Lord and show him to be one who was committed to do all that God required (see Abr. 1–3; Gen. 11:27–25:8).

Joseph Smith taught: "The word spoken to Noah was not sufficient for Abraham, or it was not required of Abraham to leave the land of his nativity and seek an inheritance in a strange country upon the word spoken to Noah. But for himself he obtained promises at the hand of the Lord and walked in [such] perfection that he was called the friend of God"[1] (see 2 Chr. 20:7; Isa. 41:8; James 2:23).

Joseph Smith also noted that Abraham "was guided in all his family affairs by the Lord; was told where to go, and when to stop; was conversed with by angels, and by the Lord; and prospered exceedingly in all that he put his hand unto." All this "was because he and his family obeyed the counsel of the Lord."[2] Abraham's desire to be obedient in all things was shown in his willingness to sacrifice that which was most precious to him in response to God's command (see Gen. 22:1–18).

In contrast, as Joseph Smith observed rhetorically, others "will set up stakes and say, 'Thus far will we go and no farther.' Did Abraham, when called upon to offer his son?"[3] As a result of his willingness to sacrifice even his long-promised child, Abraham received "power, even power of an endless life, . . . which was not the power of a prophet, nor apostle, nor patriarch only, but of [a] king and priest to God—to open the windows of heaven and pour out the peace and law of endless life to man."[4] Indeed, as we learn in modern revelation, Abraham has "entered into [his] exaltation, according to the promises," and he sits on a throne, not as an angel but as a god (D&C 132:37).

One manifestation of Abraham's greatness is that the Lord called him to become the father of a covenant family—*the* family through which all people on earth would be blessed. Among his lineal and adopted descendants the blessings of the gospel would be found, and through them those blessings would be made available to all humankind.

Modern revelation gives us an understanding of the covenant of Abraham that cannot be found in the Bible alone. We know, for example, that the Abrahamic covenant is the gospel of Jesus Christ, with its promises and ordinances. The book of Abraham in the Pearl of Great Price provides important doctrinal contributions, as do the Book of Mormon and the Doctrine and Covenants. From the Joseph Smith Translation we learn that the covenants which God made with Abraham were the same as those he had made with righteous people before Abraham's time, including Enoch, Noah, Melchizedek, and others (see Moses 7:60–64; see also Abr. 1:2–4).[5] But we identify the covenant with Abraham because the Bible and the Book of Mormon, scriptural records of his descendants, have him as a focal point of family and covenant inheritance. Faithful Saints today rejoice to be counted among his descendants and seek to follow his example of righteousness.

SACRED PROMISES

A covenant is an agreement in which two parties make commitments, each accepting certain obligations that pertain to their relationship. In a gospel covenant, we enter into sacred agreements with God, promising our obedience to his will. In turn, he has promised glorious blessings to us if we obey and serve him. The scriptures emphasize the conditional nature of covenants. If we are not faithful to our obligations, we have no claim on the promises.

Abraham committed himself unwaveringly to the Lord's service and was privileged to enter into a covenant with him. The Bible tells of the tremendous blessings that were promised to him because of his faith and obedience. The following examples are illustrative: "Lift up now thine eyes, and look from the place where thou art northward, and southward, and eastward, and westward: For all the land which thou seest, to thee will I give it, and to thy seed for ever. And I will make thy seed as the dust of the earth: so that if a man can number the dust of the earth, then shall thy seed also be numbered" (Gen. 13:14–16; see also v. 17). "And I will establish my covenant between me and thee and thy seed after thee in their generations for an everlasting covenant, to be a God unto thee, and to thy seed after thee" (Gen. 17:7). "And in thy seed shall all the nations of the earth be blessed" (Gen. 22:18).

Abraham's son and grandson Isaac and Jacob received similar promises and became subject to the same covenants and obligations that their father had received (see Gen. 26:3–4; 28:14; 35:11–12). In like manner, the covenant was renewed at Sinai with the whole house of Israel—the descendants of those three men (Ex. 19:1–8). Those who descend from Israel are blessed, by inheritance, with the same blessings and obligations that their great forefathers received. In modern times that covenant has been renewed again in the Lord's Church (see D&C 84:33–40, 48; 110:12). Thus Latter-day Saints today can rightly view the covenants of the patriarchs as being covenants between God and themselves in their own time.

The scriptures point to four major aspects of the covenant God made with the patriarchs and their descendants: a promised land, a great posterity, priesthood and gospel blessings, and a ministry of salvation to others. These blessings have both temporal and spiritual implications.

1. A promised land. The land of Canaan was given as a blessing to Abraham and his covenant children (see Gen. 13:14–15). The Lord said, "And I will give unto thee, and to thy seed after thee, the land wherein thou art a stranger, all the land of Canaan, for an everlasting possession" (Gen. 17:8). In later revelations we read of other promised lands; the Americas were given as an inheritance to the children of Joseph (see 3 Ne. 16:16; 21:22; Ether 13:8). "This is the land of your inheritance," said Jesus to the children of Lehi, "the Father hath given it unto you" (3 Ne. 15:13). Perhaps other lands were promised to others of the Lord's children who had been "led away" by him (2 Ne. 10:22).

The scriptures make it clear that the inheritance of a promised land, like every other blessing, is conditioned on the righteous behavior of the people. In the Old Testament we read how God annulled the promise of the land when his people refused to serve him. First, the ten northern tribes were taken from the land as a result of their unworthiness (see 2 Kgs. 17). Later the tribes of Judah and Benjamin were similarly taken (see 2 Kgs. 24–25).[6] Ancient Israel was denied the blessing that its people had failed to earn, all in fulfillment of the Lord's word that inheritance in the land could only be obtained on the condition of faithfulness (see Deut. 28:15, 63–64). Moses had warned them: "When thou shalt beget children, and children's children, and ye shall have remained long in the land, and shall corrupt yourselves, and make a graven image, or the likeness of any thing, and shall do evil in the sight of the Lord thy God, to provoke him to anger: I call heaven and earth to witness against you this day, that ye shall soon utterly perish from off the land whereunto ye go over Jordan to possess it; ye shall not prolong your days upon it, but shall utterly be destroyed. And the Lord shall scatter you among the nations, and ye shall be left few in number among the heathen, whither the Lord shall lead you" (Deut. 4:25–27).

Because a promised land is one of the blessings of the covenant, it is only on the stipulations of the covenant that it can be received. Consistent with this principle, the scriptures teach that Israel cannot be gathered to its promised land without accepting the gospel (Abr. 2:6; Deut. 4:29–31; 2 Ne. 6:11; 10:7–8; 25:15–16). As Jesus taught, "And it shall come to pass that the time cometh, when the fulness of my gospel shall be preached unto them; and they shall believe in me, that I am Jesus Christ, the Son of God, and shall pray unto the Father in my name. . . . Then will the Father gather them together again, and give unto them Jerusalem for the land of their inheritance" (3 Ne. 20:30–31, 33).

2. *A great posterity.* Perhaps the best-known blessing of the covenant that God made with Abraham is that of a vast number of descendants (see Gen. 13:16; 15:5; 17:4; 22:17).

Abraham was promised that his posterity would be as numerous as the dust of the earth, the sand of the seashore, and the stars of the heavens. Today one can see a partial fulfillment of this promise in the many millions of people who look upon him as their ancestor. Millions of Arabs acknowledge Abraham as their lineal parent, as do millions of Jews. We Latter-day Saints hold him as our forefather, and more than one billion other Christians and Muslims consider Abraham to be their ancestor in a less literal sense.

These figures show the earthly reality of God's promise to his faithful servant. But the ultimate realization will come in a different way. The promises "pertain to the continuation of the family unit in the highest heaven of the celestial world."[7] Modern revelation tells of the heavenly fulfillment: "Abraham received promises concerning his seed, and of the fruit of his loins . . . which were to continue so long as they were in the world; and as touching Abraham and his seed, out of the world they should continue; both in the world and out of the world should they continue as innumerable as the stars; or, if ye were to count the sand upon the seashore ye could not number them" (D&C 132:30). The Abrahamic promise of countless descendants thus pertains in its fullest sense to the eternal world following the resurrection. It is the promise of "a continuation of the family unit in eternity; of posterity in numbers as the dust of the earth and the stars in the firmament; of eternal increase."[8] With our understanding of exaltation, eternal families, and the nature of God and his work, we can catch the vision of the magnitude of the promises that the Lord made with Abraham and his covenant children.

3. Priesthood and gospel blessings. Faithful heirs of Abraham will possess the gospel and the blessings made available through the Lord's priesthood. They have a right, by virtue of their inheritance, to the priesthood and the gospel blessings that flow from it. Yet they can receive its powers and actually realize the blessing of their birthright only on the basis of their individual worthiness. Some key passages of scripture teach us the principles involved: "And in thee (that is, thy Priesthood) and in thy seed (that is, in thy Priesthood), for I give unto thee a promise that *this right shall continue in thee, and in thy seed after thee* (that is to say, the literal seed, or the seed of the body) shall all the families of the earth be blessed" (Abr. 2:11; emphasis added). Thus the right to priesthood blessings will continue with Abraham's descendants. It is their birthright, conditioned on their worthiness. In a similar passage of revelation the Lord said: "Therefore, thus saith the Lord unto you, *with whom the priesthood hath continued through the lineage of your fathers—For ye are lawful heirs, according to the flesh,* and have been hid from the world with Christ in God—Therefore your life and the priesthood have remained, and must needs remain through you and your lineage until the restoration of all things spoken by the mouths of all the holy prophets since the world began" (D&C 86:8–10; emphasis added).

4. *A ministry of salvation.* Abraham's children are called to bring salvation to others, both to Israel and to the rest of the human family. The scriptures teach that through Abraham and his descendants "shall all the families of the earth be blessed, even with the blessings of the Gospel, which are the blessings of salvation, even of life eternal" (Abr. 2:11). First and foremost among those blessings is the atoning sacrifice of Jesus Christ, a descendant of Abraham (see Matt. 1:1–16; Luke 3:23–34). Because of him, all will be saved from the bands of death and will be resurrected. All but those very few who commit the unpardonable sin will receive an eternal inheritance in a degree of glory because of Christ.

The second aspect of the Abrahamic ministry of salvation is the calling that Abraham's covenant children have received to take the gospel and its blessings to the rest of humanity. The house of Israel has been called to carry the gospel to the world. The Lord explained the following to Abraham concerning his descendants: "In their hands they shall bear this ministry and Priesthood unto all nations" (Abr. 2:9). Since the days of Abraham, Isaac, and Jacob, when gospel blessings have been available to men and women on earth, it has been through the house of Israel. Thus Abraham's children are *chosen* people—chosen to serve, chosen to bless the world through the gospel message and priesthood keys that they bear.

Those who are not of Abraham's lineage are also blessed by the Abrahamic covenant. The house of Israel is the family of the Lord's Saints, and those who accept the gospel and join the Church become members of the family, even if they are not literal descendants of the ancient patriarchs. This is in fulfilment of the words of biblical prophets (see Isa. 11:10–12; 56:6–8; Jer. 16:19–21). The Lord taught Abraham concerning the nations of the earth who were not his physical offspring: "And I will bless them through thy name; for as many as receive this Gospel shall be called after thy name, and shall be accounted thy seed, and shall rise up and bless thee, as their father" (Abr. 2:10). Paul taught the same doctrine concerning non-Israelites who accept the gospel: "For as many of you as have been baptized into Christ have put on Christ. There is neither Jew nor Greek [i.e., neither Israelite nor non-Israelite], there is neither bond nor free, there is neither male nor female: for ye are all one in Christ Jesus. And if ye be Christ's, then are ye Abraham's seed, and heirs according to the promise" (Gal. 3:27–29).

By the principle of adoption, non-Israelites who accept the

gospel are brought into the family and are accounted heirs of the covenant. They *become* members of the house of Israel, in which there is no distinction between those who are the literal seed of Abraham and those who become his heirs through adoption, for they are "all one in Christ Jesus" (Gal. 3:28). Patriarchal blessings identify them with one of the tribes of Israel, and they are heirs to all the promises and responsibilities.

THE COVENANT PEOPLE OF THE LORD

In the last days the Lord has called the covenant children of the ancient patriarchs "a light unto the Gentiles, and through this priesthood, a savior unto my people Israel" (D&C 86:11). The two-fold calling of the latter-day children of Abraham, Isaac, and Jacob is to gather others of the house of Israel back to the covenants and to gather as well all others who desire to become one with them. What we call the Abrahamic Covenant is the fulness of the gospel of Jesus Christ, and it is available to all. It has been restored anew in modern times for the blessing of all people. Every faithful man and woman can receive its blessings to the fullest degree by accepting baptismal and temple covenants and by living faithfully. Elder Bruce R. McConkie taught:

"These are the promises made to the fathers. Is not it a marvelous thing that God himself said to Abraham, to Isaac, and to Jacob, and then to Joseph Smith, that in them and their seed all generations should be blessed? This is the promise of eternal increase. Would we suppose that there is anyone else in the world in addition to Joseph Smith in our day who ever received that promise? . . . Let us catch the vision of what is involved here. The Lord does not give blessings to Abraham,

Isaac, and Jacob, and to the President of the Church, that are not available to every faithful elder and sister. It does not make one particle of difference what one's position is. Everything comes on the basis of personal righteousness: everyone in the Church who has been married in the temple has received exactly the same promise that God gave to Abraham, Isaac, and Jacob."[9]

Several scriptures emphasize the conditional nature of God's selection of the house of Israel, and those passages remind us of our individual need for personal worthiness. Nephi taught that had the Canaanites in the promised land been as righteous as the Israelites, Israel would not have been "more choice" in God's eyes than they (1 Ne. 17:34). "The Lord esteemeth all flesh in one," Nephi said, and "he that is righteous is favored of God" (1 Ne. 17:35). Later he stated, "As many of the Gentiles as will repent are the covenant people of the Lord; and as many of the Jews as will not repent shall be cast off; for the Lord covenanteth with none save it be with them that repent and believe in his Son, who is the Holy One of Israel" (2 Ne. 30:2).

Latter-day Saints are privileged to live in a time when covenant blessings are available and the promises made to ancient progenitors are being fulfilled. Faithful Saints such as Abraham, who has already gone on to receive his eternal reward (see D&C 132:37), set a pattern for us to follow.

NOTES

1. Dean C. Jessee, ed., *Autobiographical and Historical Writings,* vol. 1 of *The Personal Writings of Joseph Smith* series (Salt Lake City: Deseret Book, 1984–), 298; capitalization and punctuation standardized.

2. *Times and Seasons,* 15 July 1842, 857.

3. Andrew F. Ehat and Lyndon W. Cook, eds., *The Words of Joseph Smith: The Contemporary Accounts of the Nauvoo Discourses of the Prophet Joseph* (Provo, Utah: Religious Studies Center, Brigham Young University, 1980), 246; capitalization and punctuation standardized.

4. Ibid., 245; capitalization and punctuation standardized.

5. *I.V.* Gen. 8:23; 9:15, 17, 21–23; 14:26–34.

6. Israel (the northern tribes) was deported 734–721 B.C., and Judah (Judah and Benjamin) was deported in 597 and 587 B.C. and some thereafter.

7. Bruce R. McConkie, *The Millennial Messiah: The Second Coming of the Son of Man* (Salt Lake City: Deseret Book, 1982), 262.

8. Ibid., 267.

9. McConkie, "The Promises Made to the Fathers," in *Genesis to 2 Samuel,* ed. Kent P. Jackson and Robert L. Millet, vol. 3 in *Studies in Scripture* series (Salt Lake City: Deseret Book, 1989), 60.

12

MATRIARCHS AND PATRIARCHS

AS THE PROPHET JOSEPH SMITH labored on his New Translation of Genesis, he made many changes in early chapters (Genesis 1–9, 14) and in two of the last chapters (Genesis 48, 50). Although he made fewer changes in between, they are still informative, and some have important doctrinal implications. The book of Abraham contributes also in significant ways to our understanding of the generations of Abraham, Isaac, and Jacob.

Abram and Sarai were natives of a place called Ur of the Chaldees, located in northern Mesopotamia in an area rich in interaction between cultures.[1] Not far away was Haran, also called Aram-Naharaim and Padan-aram (see Gen. 24:10; 28:5–6), a place that in the Bible is known as the family's homeland (see Gen. 24:4) and the source from which the mothers of Israel—Rebekah, Leah, Rachel, Bilhah, and Zilpah—would come.[2] It is not unlikely that Sarai and Abram were blood relatives, in keeping with a common custom of the time to marry within the extended family. In one passage Abram states that Sarai was "the daughter of [his] father, but

not the daughter of [his] mother" (Gen. 20:12). Modern revelation clarifies that while they were in Egypt, Abram was
instructed by God to have Sarai identify herself as his sister,
rather than as his spouse, as a means of saving his life (see Abr.
2:22–25; Gen. 12:9–15; 20).[3]

Some time after their marriage, Abram and Sarai showed
their obedience to the Lord's wishes by leaving forever their
homeland and traveling to a new country hundreds of miles
distant (see Abr. 1:16; 2:3, 6, 14–16). Haran was but a stop on
the way, for Canaan would be their promised land. It would
belong not only to them but to their descendants also, on the
terms of the covenant that the Lord would establish with
them—"when they hearken to my voice" (Abr. 2:6).

Through the Restoration we know that Abram, Sarai, and
their family members possessed a knowledge of the gospel of
Jesus Christ. During his mortal ministry, Jesus was confronted
by Pharisees with the challenge that he made himself greater
than Abraham and the prophets. He responded, "Your father
Abraham rejoiced to see my day: and he saw it, and was glad"
(John 8:56). Missing from the Old Testament is any reference
to Abram's Christianity or to his foreseeing the days of Jesus.
But the Joseph Smith Translation at Genesis 15:6 adds an
important passage: "And it came to pass, that Abram looked
forth and saw the days of the Son of man, and was glad, and
his soul found rest, and he believed in the Lord; and the Lord
counted it unto him for righteousness."[4]

The great emphasis that Genesis places on covenant making shows the importance of covenants in the lives of believers.
Abram and Sarai, in response to their faithfulness, were given
new names: "Behold, my covenant is with thee, and thou shalt
be a father of many nations. Neither shall thy name any more
be called Abram, but thy name shall be Abraham; for a father

of many nations have I made thee" (Gen. 17:4–5). And "as for Sarai thy wife, thou shalt not call her name Sarai, but Sarah shall her name be. . . . I will bless her, and she shall be a mother of nations; kings of people shall be of her" (Gen. 17:15–16). The new names probably mean basically the same as the old names.[5] But the changes are important because the new names represent the new relationship that existed within the covenant between God and our faithful parents.

LOT IN SODOM

After they entered Canaan, Abraham and his nephew Lot found it necessary to divide the land between them. Lot chose to live in the Jordan Valley among the inhabitants of the "cities of the plain" (Gen. 13:12; see also vv. 5–11). Abraham's residence was the hill country to the west of the Jordan Rift Valley. By means of the Joseph Smith Translation, modern revelation adds interesting information to the account of Lot's experiences among the people of Sodom. Genesis 14 tells how five kings invaded the land together, defeated the local kings, plundered their land, and took both booty and captives as they left. Among the captives was Lot. Abraham, "the man of God," mobilized his forces to rescue his kinsman. His army consisted of 318 men, including "his trained men, and they which were born in his own house." With this armed force, Abraham went after the kings and defeated them in battle. He "brought back Lot, his brother's son, and all his goods, and the women also, and the people" (JST at Gen. 14:13–14, 16[6]). It was on his return from the battle that Abraham was met by Melchizedek, king of Salem.[7]

Lot resumed his residence in Sodom. This was not a fortunate choice, however, because although Sodom survived the invasion of the kings, it would not survive the judgments of God. When Abraham learned from three messengers that Sodom and Gomorrah would be destroyed, he again found himself needing to save Lot. Demonstrating his concern for his nephew and his family, he pleaded with the Lord to spare the city if even only ten righteous people could be found in it (see Gen. 18:22–33). But in the end, ten righteous people could not be found. Lot, his wife, and his two daughters were able to leave, but the city and the rest of its inhabitants were destroyed. Joseph Smith taught that the destruction of Sodom and Gomorrah resulted from their rejection of the gospel and the prophets who taught it: "In consequence of rejecting the gospel of Jesus Christ and the prophets whom God has sent, the judgments of God have rested upon people, cities, and nations in various ages of the world, which was the case with the cities of Sodom and Gomorrah, who were destroyed for rejecting the prophets."[8]

The Joseph Smith Translation adds a few clarifications to the account of the rescue of Lot's family. When the wicked men of the city wanted Lot to surrender his guests, "that we may know them" (Gen. 19:5), the Bible has Lot perversely offering instead his two daughters (see Gen. 19:8). The Joseph Smith Translation explains that the citizens demanded both the visitors and the daughters, but Lot refused both. All of this evil, the Joseph Smith Translation adds, "was after the wickedness of Sodom."[9]

CIRCUMCISION AND BAPTISM

God renewed his covenant with Abraham (see Gen. 17:1–9) and instituted circumcision as the sign of the covenant. The Joseph Smith Translation supplies two significant additions to the text. The first is a statement from the Lord regarding the apostasy of his people: "My people have gone astray from my precepts, and have not kept mine ordinances, which I gave unto their fathers; and they have not observed mine anointing, and the burial, or baptism wherewith I commanded them; but have turned from the commandment, and taken unto themselves the washing of children, and the blood of sprinkling; and have said that the blood of the righteous Abel was shed for sins; and have not known wherein they are accountable before me" (I.V. Gen. 17:4–7). Rather than describing pagan nations who never knew the truth, these verses describe people who once had been favored with the gospel but had perverted its doctrines and ordinances. Among other things, they had changed the ordinance of the *burial* through baptism to a *washing* of children and "the blood of *sprinkling*."[10] In addition to this they had changed the doctrine of the atonement of Jesus Christ to a doctrine of redemption through the blood of Abel. Outside of a puzzling reference in Hebrews 12:24, this idea is not found elsewhere in scripture. It must have been a common doctrine among apostates of Abraham's day.

Genesis 17 is the first mention in the Old Testament of the ordinance of circumcision, the surgical removal of the skin on the front part of the male sex organ. This practice was given to Abraham to be the token of the covenant established between him and God. In modern societies it is common to wear clothing decorated with words or symbols to represent things with which we choose to identify ourselves. The token of the Abrahamic covenant, which was incised into the flesh of the believer, was not for public display but for a personal reminder. An inspired Joseph Smith Translation addition at Genesis 17:7 gives further insight into the purpose of this ordinance: "And I will establish a covenant of circumcision with thee, and it shall be my covenant between me and thee, and thy seed after thee, in their generations; that thou mayest know for ever that children are not accountable before me until they are eight years old."[11] It is clear from the passages in the Joseph Smith Translation cited above that the concepts of baptism, redemption, and accountability were distorted in Abraham's day. Circumcision, administered when a male child was eight days old, not only was a sign that the child was born into the covenant of Abraham but also showed that he was born free of sin and was unaccountable until eight years old,[12] when he would receive baptism for the remission of sins—a sign of his taking part in the redemptive work of the Lord Jesus Christ.[13]

SARAH, HAGAR, AND ABRAHAM

When Sarah is first introduced in Genesis, we are told that she was barren (see Gen. 11:30). This information is intended to be neither insignificant nor demeaning but is fundamental to the narrative because of the miraculous birth that would take place many years later. Before the birth of Isaac, both Sarah and Abraham are described as being "old and well stricken in age," and Sarah was beyond natural child-bearing years (Gen. 18:11; see also v. 12). Their frustration, or confusion, over their childless state certainly must have been intensified as a result of the Lord's frequent promises that they would have a large posterity (e.g., Gen. 13:16; 15:5; 17:4). Sarah did not disbelieve the promises, as is evident from her actions, but after a lifetime of being unable to conceive children, and now seemingly being too old to do so, she proposed a solution that she felt would enable the prophecies to be fulfilled. She encouraged Abraham to marry her servant Hagar, "that I may obtain children by her" (Gen. 16:2). Sarah owned Hagar, and thus any children born to Hagar's union with Abraham would be Sarah's. A revelation to Joseph Smith makes the matter more clear: "God commanded Abraham, and Sarah gave Hagar to Abraham to wife" (D&C 132:34). This marriage resulted in the birth of Abraham's son Ishmael and in an entire lineage of Abraham's descendants. "From Hagar sprang many people. This, therefore, was fulfilling, among other things, the promises" (D&C 132:34). Like Abraham's Israelite offspring, the descendants of Ishmael—the Arabs—are promised children who help fulfill God's covenant to Abraham.

Genesis records the coming to Abraham and Sarah of three men who had been sent to give them an important message. The text is not altogether clear about the identity of the three, because they are called both "men" and "angels" (Gen. 18:2; 19:1). Moreover, the text in a few places presents God speaking as though he were one of the three (see Gen. 18:10, 13[14]; cf. 18:1; 21:1). The Joseph Smith Translation changes "the men" to "the angels which were holy men" (at Gen. 18:22) and to "the angels of God, which were holy men" (at Gen. 19:10). Elsewhere it calls the visitors "angels" (at Gen. 21:1; see also v. 2), and Joseph Smith referred to them as "angels."[15] But perhaps the obviously deliberate reference to their eating (see Gen. 18:5–8) is intended to inform us that they were mortals and not angelic beings and that "angels" is meant to be understood in its original sense (both in English and in Hebrew) as "messengers." The message of the three visitors was that Sarah and Abraham would at last have a child. Despite the age of the future parents, nothing is "too hard for the Lord." And indeed through Sarah, "Abraham shall surely become a great and mighty nation" (Gen. 18:14, 18).

Some years after the birth of the promised son, Isaac, the faith of his parents was tested again when Abraham was commanded to sacrifice him as an offering to the Lord (see Gen.

22:1–19). To this event modern revelation adds a context that is completely unknown in the Bible. In the book of Abraham we learn that Abraham himself, many years earlier, had been the intended victim of a human sacrifice at the instigation of his own father (Abr. 1:5–17, 30). Although Abraham knew that the attempt to sacrifice him had been motivated by the worship of false gods, still the command to sacrifice his own son must have evoked feelings in his heart that we can only imagine. That he was willing to obey, despite his memory of the past event, emphasizes even more powerfully the nobility of his character. His action was, as the Book of Mormon prophet Jacob said, "a similitude of God and his Only Begotten Son" (Jacob 4:5). Abraham's faithfulness to the Lord's command assured his blessings. As Joseph Smith taught, Abraham obtained "power, even power of an endless life, . . . by the offering of his son Isaac, which was not the power of a prophet, nor apostle, nor patriarch only, but of [a] king and priest to God—to open the windows of heaven and pour out the peace and law of endless life to man."[16] Indeed, "if a man would attain—he must sacrifice all to attain to the keys of the kingdom of an endless life."[17]

The focus in the Old Testament is on Abraham's descendants through Sarah's son, Isaac, and Isaac's son Jacob. Through that lineage, a unique and special covenant relationship would continue. But we know also that from other marriages Abraham had additional children. His son Ishmael became the father of twelve tribes. Abraham and his wife Keturah, whom he apparently married after the death of Sarah, had six sons and perhaps daughters also. Many years later, the Bible introduces us to Jethro, a descendant of Abraham and Keturah (see Gen. 25:1–6, 12–18; Ex. 2:16–21; 3:1). Unlike the Israelites of his generation, who had lost their knowledge of the gospel in Egypt, Jethro had the gospel and held the Melchizedek Priesthood. Presumably these had been passed down through his faithful progenitors since the days of their father Abraham. Indeed, Moses probably learned of the gospel and was converted to it only when he came into contact with Jethro in the land of Midian. There he married Jethro's daughter and received under Jethro's hands his ordination to the Melchizedek Priesthood (see D&C 84:6–13, 23–27).

We learn through modern revelation that Abraham's marriages were not only in harmony with the Lord's will but were also eternal marriages, sealed by the power of the holy priesthood under the new and everlasting covenant. The Lord told Joseph Smith: "Abraham received all things, whatsoever he received, by revelation and commandment, by my word, saith the Lord. . . . Abraham received concubines, and they bore him children; and it was accounted unto him for righteousness, because they were given unto him, and he abode in my law" (D&C 132:29, 37). Lest anyone assume incorrectly, a concubine was a wife, but she was a wife who in the culture of the day did not enjoy the legal status of a free woman, usually being a servant like Hagar, or like Bilhah and Zilpah, the wives of Jacob.

REBEKAH, LEAH, RACHEL, BILHAH, AND ZILPAH

The Joseph Smith Translation makes only a very few minor changes in the records of Isaac and Jacob and their families. The Restoration reveals few new details for those chapters, and thus our discussion will be limited to some general principles. But the restored gospel does provide a background that is not clearly visible in the Bible. That background is the eternal nature of family units sealed by the power of the holy priesthood. From reading the Genesis text, one might conclude that the desire to seek a certain kind of wife and the desire to have children reflect only the ancient Near Eastern culture of biblical times. But through the Restoration, we learn principles concerning families that have motivated believers in the true God in every generation.

The gospel teaches us to marry within our faith. Genesis emphasizes the importance of doing so by recording the efforts to obtain suitable wives for Isaac and Jacob. It appears that for some time following the translation of the community of Melchizedek, the pool of believers where Abraham lived in Canaan may have been somewhat limited.[18] Like modern Latter-day Saints in a similar situation, Abraham wanted his son to marry a righteous woman who worshiped the true God. A polytheist Canaanite would not be acceptable. Thus he sent his servant to Aram-naharaim, the ancestral home Haran, and instructed him to find a wife there for Isaac (see Gen. 24). In the next generation, Isaac and Rebekah grieved that their son Esau married two Hittite women (see Gen. 26:34–35). Wanting their son Jacob to marry in their religion, they sent him also to the land of Haran to find a wife among his mother's family. Eventually Jacob married two sisters who were his first cousins, as well as two other women. These four became the mothers of the twelve tribes of Israel (see Gen. 27:46; 28:1–30:43).

In these two unique cases, it is unlikely that the nationality or ethnicity of potential wives was at issue. Abraham's wife Hagar was an Egyptian (see Gen. 16:1). His wife Keturah was presumably from Canaan where he lived (see Gen. 25:1–6). The Bible tells us that Joseph's wife, the mother of Ephraim and Manasseh, was an Egyptian also (see Gen. 41:50–52). While we know very little of the background of these women, we have every reason to believe that all these marriages were within the faith and that the wives were righteous and worthy believers in the God of Abraham, Isaac, and Jacob.[19]

Even a casual reading shows that a major theme of Genesis is the desire for children, a desire that influences much of the narrative in the three generations from Abraham to Jacob. In the ancient Near East, children were a valued asset. Sons were particularly important for the economic well-being of the family, for the perpetuation of ownership of ancestral property, and for the care of parents in their old age. The Bible shows that infertility was viewed as a cause for much grief. Undoubtedly its implications were especially felt by an infertile wife in a polygamous marriage. The gospel teaches us of the permanence of the relationship between parent and child, and living the gospel develops divinely inherited instincts that lead us to desire offspring. As a consequence, Latter-day Saints throughout their history have had more children than were normative in society, and it is likely that Saints in other generations have also placed a high value on families.[20] But not all have been able to have the families they desired. In Genesis, Sarah's barrenness is followed by that of her daughter-in-law, Rebekah. In the next generation, Rebekah's daughter-in-law Rachel is barren also. In all three cases eventual conception and birth were viewed as acts of divine intervention in response to much pleading and prayer (see Gen. 25:20–26; 29:31; 30:1–2, 22–23).

In the ancient world, where literature was often created to aggrandize the ruling family, this part of Genesis stands out as a work of profound honesty that does not always present its family in a flattering light. It candidly sets before us its story, even if doing so exposes imperfections in the people whose lives are recounted in it. Thus we learn of struggles in relationships that developed over such things as property, marriages, inheritances, child-bearing, and unfulfilled hopes and needs.

Like us, the ancestors of the house of Israel were humans who sometimes responded to life in very human ways.[21] Yet in reading Genesis, we should keep in mind that we do not have a complete account of the matriarchs and patriarchs but only a record of some key events that shaped their lives. Perhaps some of these events are in the Bible because they are the exceptions, rather than the rule. Nor do we understand fully the challenges they faced, the realities of their culture, and the assumptions and beliefs that formed their society. The inspired author of Genesis presented the story with honesty and without either judgment or rationalization. God is shown to be aware of the weaknesses that plague all humans, and he appears to be more patient with them than we sometimes are. He was especially mindful of those whose circumstances in life were particularly hard. In cases where it seems that injustice was done—even by good men and women—God compensated for it by providing extra blessings for those who had been adversely affected (see Gen. 16:3–10; 21:9–21; 29:30–35; 31:10–12). Jehovah is the great Equalizer in these stories, foreshadowing how his atonement will ultimately level life's playing field for all people. Perhaps one message of Genesis is that God chose the family of Abraham and worked through them to accomplish his purposes, despite whatever weaknesses they may have had, just as we hope he will do with us.

The lives of the matriarchs and patriarchs are examples to us of faithfulness and courage. When Abraham's servant went to Haran to find a wife for Isaac, Rebekah showed tremendous faith in her willing departure from home and family to marry a man she did not know (see Gen. 24:1–67). When she was asked her desire, she replied, "I will go." In response, her family blessed her and said, "Thou art our sister, be thou the mother of thousands of millions" (Gen. 24:58, 60). Years later, Rebekah showed great wisdom and courage when her husband intended to give his chief blessing to Esau rather than to Jacob. Knowing through personal revelation that Jacob was to receive the blessing, she guided the situation carefully and assured that the prophecy was fulfilled in accordance with the Lord's will (see Gen. 27:1–29). Abraham and Jacob are examples of obedient people who hastened to do what the Lord commanded them (see Abr. 2:3–4; Gen. 22:1–3; 31:3, 17–18; 35:1–5). Leah and Rachel were quick to say, "Whatsoever God hath said unto thee, do," even when it meant leaving forever their parents and homeland (Gen. 31:16). Concerning Isaac, Joseph Smith said, "He was more holy and more perfect before God and came to him with a purer heart and more faith than men in this day."[22] And Abraham's wife Hagar was twice visited by an angel, who gave her comfort and foretold the future (see Gen. 16:7–14; 21:17–18).

Modern revelation tells us where these great people are now: Abraham "hath entered into his exaltation and sitteth upon his throne," and Isaac and Jacob "have entered into their exaltation, according to the promises, and sit upon thrones, and are not angels but are gods" (D&C 132:29, 37). Since exaltation comes to couples and not just to husbands, then certainly the wives of Abraham, Isaac, and Jacob are with them in their glory. And we have every reason to believe that among them are not only those who were favored in this life—Sarah, Rebekah, and Rachel—but also the wives who were loved less or were called handmaids or concubines or concerning whom little is made known in Genesis—including Hagar, Keturah, Leah, Bilhah, and Zilpah.

NOTES

1. Many maps locate Ur of the Chaldees in southern Mesopotamia, following an identification popularized in the early twentieth century.

Most Latter-day Saint scholars who have researched the location of Ur recognize that the southern location is inconsistent with the scriptural text, particularly the book of Abraham, whereas the northern location fits the evidence. See Paul Y. Hoskisson, "Where Was Ur of the Chaldees?" in *The Pearl of Great Price: Revelations From God,* ed. H. Donl Peterson and Charles D. Tate Jr. (Provo, Utah: Religious Studies Center, Brigham Young University, 1989), 119–36; John M. Lundquist, "Was Abraham at Ebla? A Cultural Background of the Book of Abraham," in *The Pearl of Great Price,* ed. Robert L. Millet and Kent P. Jackson, vol. 2 of *Studies in Scripture* series (Salt Lake City: Randall Book, 1985), 225–37; and John Gee and Stephen D. Ricks, "Historical Plausibility: The Historicity of the Book of Abraham as a Case Study," in *Historicity and the Latter-day Saint Scriptures,* ed. Paul Y. Hoskisson (Provo, Utah: Religious Studies Center, Brigham Young University, 2001), 70–72.

2. Aram-Naharaim means "Syria of the Two Rivers." It is rendered "Mesopotamia" in the King James translation (see Gen. 24:10).

3. In the first printing of the book of Abraham text in 1842, both Sarah and Nahor's wife Milcah were identified as "the daughters of Haran," the brother of Nahor and Abraham, making Sarah Abraham's niece. That reading remained in all subsequent editions (at Abr. 2:2) until the edition of 1981, which identifies only Milcah as Haran's daughter. See *Times and Seasons,* 1 March 1842, 705.

4. I.V. Genesis 15:12. "I.V." references are to the chapter and verse numbers in the printed *Inspired Version.*

5. *Abram* means "(The Divine) Father Is Exalted." *Abraham* is generally considered to be an expanded form of the same name. *Sarai* is probably an archaic form of *Sarah,* "Ruler (f.)."

6. I.V. Genesis 14:12, 13, 15.

7. See chapter 10 of this book.

8. Andrew F. Ehat and Lyndon W. Cook, eds., *The Words of Joseph Smith: The Contemporary Accounts of the Nauvoo Discourses of the Prophet Joseph* (Provo, Utah: Religious Studies Center, Brigham Young University, 1980), 156; capitalization, punctuation, and grammar standardized.

9. I.V. Genesis 19:12; see also vv. 9–11, 13–32.

10. I.V. Genesis 17:6. Baptism, according to the scriptures, is not a representation of *washing* but of *death, burial,* and *rebirth* (Rom. 6:3–4; Eph. 4:22–24; Col. 2:12; 3:1–2). Thus sprinkling cannot be a valid

ordinance, because it cannot represent those factors that are brought to bear when spiritual rebirth and its associated ordinance (baptism) take place.

11. *I.V.* Genesis 17:11.

12. This is the first mention of the age of accountability in modern revelation, coming in February or March of 1831. The revelation recorded in the Doctrine and Covenants that gives eight years as the age of accountability (see D&C 68:25) came eight or nine months later (November 1831).

13. Israelite women had no such sign of their membership in the covenant family, but they nonetheless shared in its blessings. Circumcision was in force until the mortal ministry of Jesus, when it was (and continued to be) no longer required of members of the Lord's Church (see Acts 15:1–29; Gal. 3:27–29; 6:15; D&C 74; see also Rom. 6:4).

14. "The LORD" translates the Hebrew divine name *Yahweh*.

15. Dean C. Jessee, ed., *The Personal Writings of Joseph Smith* (Salt Lake City: Deseret Book, 1984), 247.

16. Ehat and Cook, eds., *Words of Joseph Smith*, 245; capitalization and punctuation standardized.

17. Ibid., 244.

18. Joseph Smith wrote: "Abraham [came] with knowledge, or revelation, and what is the result? Why he becomes a pilgrim in a strange land; no body believed in his religion because he had new revelations." *Times and Seasons*, 15 August 1842, 890.

19. The wives of Jacob's other sons were probably mostly local women from Canaan (see Gen. 38:1–2, 12; 46:10).

20. Tim B. Heaton, "Vital Statistics," in Daniel H. Ludlow, ed., *Encyclopedia of Mormonism* (New York: Macmillan, 1992), 1521–24; Tim B. Heaton, "Religious Influences on Mormon Fertility: Cross-National Comparisons," *Review of Religious Research* 30, no. 4 (June 1989): 401–11.

21. The frankness with which Genesis presents such things testifies to the historicity of what it records.

22. Jessee, ed., *Personal Writings of Joseph Smith*, 299.

13

JACOB AND THE HOUSE OF GOD

THE OLD TESTAMENT TELLS THE STORY of a relationship between a family and its god. The god was Jehovah, and the family was the house of Israel. Genesis, the beginning of the family history, is a book about the covenants that were made between Jehovah and that family—covenants that bound the two parties in a relationship of mutual trust and obligation. Among the promises that God made to our ancestors are not only those that are emphasized in the Bible—land and earthly posterity—but also others that we encounter through modern revelation, and particularly in our temples, that have profound implications both now and in the eternities.

AT BETH-EL AND PENIEL

Jacob's life history was punctuated with spiritual experiences that are among the most powerful recorded in scripture. The first of these happened as he was on his way to Haran to find a wife. Jacob stopped at a place called Luz, where two generations earlier his grandfather Abraham had built an altar and prayed (see Gen. 12:8; Abr. 2:20). The text tells us only that it was dark and that Jacob decided to spend the night there, perhaps unaware that he was lodging on ground that had been sanctified by Abraham's earlier worship. That night Jacob "dreamed," or as we would say, he saw a vision. He saw a ladder extending from earth to heaven. Angels were going up and down upon it, and the Lord himself stood at the top. Repeating promises that he had made to Jacob's father and grandfather, the Lord told Jacob that the land would belong to him and his descendants. He promised him a large posterity that would extend in all directions, and he told him, as he had his fathers, that in him and his seed would "all the families of the earth be blessed" (Gen. 28:14; see also vv. 11–13). At the end of his vision Jacob exclaimed: "Surely the Lord is in this place. . . . This is none other but the house of God, and this is the gate of heaven." He called the place "Beth-el"—meaning "House of God" (Gen. 28:19; see also vv. 16–17)—and it remained a sacred location among his descendants throughout the Old Testament.[1]

The Lord told Jacob that he would both "keep" him and bring him back to his homeland (Gen. 28:15). During the years Jacob lived in Haran, God's divine keeping power caused him to increase; he married four wives and eventually fathered twelve sons and some daughters (see Gen. 37:35; 46:7). His material possessions grew similarly. Then after twenty years in the area of Haran, Jacob was reminded by an angel that God was the source of his prosperity, and he was told that it was at last time for him to return to his home (see Gen. 31:3, 10–12). While he was on his way to his native land, "the angels of God" met him (Gen. 32:1). Because the word *angel* means "messenger," there must have been a message, but we are not told what it was.

Jacob's next great recorded spiritual experience came as he approached Canaan: "And Jacob was left alone; and there wrestled a man with him until the breaking of the day. . . . And he said, Let me go, for the day breaketh. And he said, I will not let thee go, except thou bless me. And he said unto him, What is thy name? And he said, Jacob. And he said, Thy name shall be called no more Jacob, but Israel: for thou hast persevered with God and with men,[2] and hast prevailed. And Jacob asked him, and said, Tell me, I pray thee, thy name. And he said, Wherefore is it that thou dost ask after my name? And he blessed him there. And Jacob called the name of the place Peniel: for I have seen God face to face, and my life is preserved" (Gen. 32:24, 26–30). The name *Peniel* means "Face of God."

It appears that the author of Genesis chose to write about this experience with such reserve that he left many things about it deliberately unclear and unspecific. At the same time, it seems that the text was not preserved intact through the centuries of its transmission. Like Jacob's vision of the ladder extending into heaven, this experience is not elaborated in modern scripture, and the Joseph Smith Translation provides no new information about it. Yet in the Beth-el and Peniel events are messages that Latter-day Saints, enlightened by the restored gospel, can understand differently than do other readers. Nowhere in Genesis or in the Old Testament, for example, can we learn what it means that all nations will be blessed through the seed of Jacob. But we know through the Restoration that in Christ, the ultimate Seed of Jacob, salvation is made available to all humankind. And we know that the calling of the house of Israel is to bless all nations by taking them the gospel with its exalting covenants and ordinances. Nor can we understand from the Old Testament what it means that

Israel's descendants would be in number "as the dust of the earth" (Gen. 28:14). But through modern revelation we learn of eternal families and eternal progeny and of the divine powers available in our temples that make those blessings possible. Indeed, the promises of Genesis include redemption through a Savior, sealings in the temple to form eternal families, and everlasting life in the presence of God.[3] The ladder in Jacob's vision likely represents the steps in our quest to obtain those blessings as we move forward through life's experiences and the covenants and ordinances of the house of the Lord. Elder Marion G. Romney suggested the following:

"Jacob realized that the covenants he made with the Lord there were the rungs on the ladder that he himself would have to climb in order to obtain the promised blessings—blessings that would entitle him to enter heaven and associate with the Lord.

"Because he had met the Lord and entered into covenants with him there, Jacob considered the site so sacred that he named the place Bethel [House of God]. . . .

"Jacob not only passed through the gate of heaven, but by living up to every covenant he also went all the way in. Of him and his forebears Abraham and Isaac, the Lord has said: ' . . . because they did none other things than that which they were commanded, they have entered into their exaltation, according to the promises, and sit upon thrones, and are not angels but are gods.' (D&C 132:37.)

"Temples are to us all what Bethel was to Jacob."[4]

If the temple is the place where heaven and earth meet, as the ladder of Beth-el was in Jacob's vision, then Jacob's wrestling at Peniel was a companion experience and a further step in his celestial curriculum. Perhaps this is suggested in the fact that the one event took place as he was leaving home and the other as he was returning, the first as a young single man and the second as the husband of women who would be his eternal companions. In the experience at Peniel, elements of a heavenly encounter are apparent, even if only hinted or disguised in the text: It was night, and the event came to a climax with the coming of the dawn; Jacob was "left alone" yet he wrestled with someone; like his grandparents Abram and Sarai, he received a new name, symbolizing his new relationship with God in the covenant; Jacob received a blessing that was worth all his exertions; and he testified that he had "seen God face to face." Whether through the author's careful use of symbolic language or through inaccuracies in the transmission of the text, we are left to wonder about the identity of the man with whom Jacob wrestled. Was it God, an angel, or a mortal? We can perhaps find it unlikely that any wrestling took place at all, and extremely unlikely that a mortal would wrestle with an angel or with God. Perhaps it was another mortal, standing in the place of God, who was sent to represent him in giving Jacob his blessings.[5]

AT BETH-EL AGAIN

After Jacob entered his promised land, the Lord commanded him to return to Beth-el, the place where he had seen the ladder ascending into heaven (see Gen. 35:1–15). To prepare for the experience there, Jacob instructed the members of his household to put away their idols, to be clean, and to change their clothing. As they traveled to the south, "the terror of God was upon the cities that were round about them" (Gen. 35:5), indicating that the Lord was accompanying them in their journey and perhaps also indicating that their repentance and purification were acknowledged. At Beth-el, God appeared to Jacob "and blessed him" (Gen. 35:9). Then he reiterated Jacob's name change and confirmed the promises he had already made of a vast posterity and of his family's possession of the land of Canaan. Jacob constructed an altar there and made an offering to the Lord.

As is the case with his other sacred experiences, this event at Beth-el is recounted in only a few brief verses with very little detail. Although Jacob is the only mortal mentioned in the narrative when God appeared, his instructing of his family members to purify and prepare themselves suggests that at some point in the experience they were participants. We know through modern revelation that Jacob received the temple ordinance of a marriage sealed for time and all eternity, because that is a prerequisite for exaltation (see D&C 132:37). If his earlier solitary visits at Beth-el and Peniel were temple experiences in which he entered into covenants with the Lord and received promises in return, then perhaps this second Beth-el experience was the crowning event in which Jacob, his wives, and his worthy children were sealed together in eternal families.

NOTES

1. The Joseph Smith Translation makes only one small change in the text of Genesis 28, in which verse 22 reads, in part: "And *the place of* this stone which I have set for a pillar, shall be *the place of* God's house."

2. Alternate reading from the Latter-day Saint edition of the King James Version, note 28c. The King James translators seem to have misunderstood the Hebrew verb.

3. See chapter 11 of this book.

4. Marion G. Romney, "Temples—The Gates to Heaven," *Ensign,* March 1971, 16.

5. This was the position of Joseph Fielding Smith, *Doctrines of Salvation,* comp. Bruce R. McConkie, 3 vols. (Salt Lake City: Bookcraft, 1954–56), 1:17.

14

JOSEPH AND THE PROMISES

MODERN REVELATION CONTRIBUTES only in limited ways to our understanding of Joseph's amazing life, but it contributes volumes to our understanding of his mission—a mission that to a large extent would be fulfilled through his descendants. In Genesis the life of Joseph receives more discussion than that of any person but Abraham. Yet the Joseph Smith Translation makes only three tiny changes in the text until the final chapters, in which great prophetic blessings are enlarged substantially.[1] That ancient Joseph was a remarkable man is shown in his receiving at a tender age revelations that foretold aspects of his future (see Gen. 37:5–11). In the record of his life in Genesis, nothing is wasted. His dreams and interpretations are not distractions or diversions from the narrative, but each one plays an important role in the carefully crafted account. This is especially true with respect to his dreams, which reveal things not only about his own lifetime but also about the role his family would play in God's work in the future. Today's Latter-day Saints have a particular need to read about Joseph and to learn of his life and ministry.

"AND THE LORD WAS WITH JOSEPH"

Even though he was the eleventh son of his father, Joseph was the birthright child, or the "firstborn," of the family. The Hebrew word translated "firstborn," *běkôr,* does not include any reference to numerical order or even to being born. In most cases the word seems to denote one who was born first, but in some instances the term was used for others who received the status of chief heir by designation.[2] Deriving from *běkôr* is the noun *běkōrâ,* meaning "birthright," or "right of the chief heir." The birthright carried benefits—but mostly obligations and expectations—that set the recipient apart from his siblings. According to Chronicles, Joseph received the birthright when Reuben, the eldest son, forfeited it by committing fornication with his father's wife (1 Chr. 5:1–2). It is sometimes suggested that when the first son of the first wife (Reuben) lost his birthright, it automatically went to the first son of the second wife (Joseph). But no such rule or precedent is found in the Bible, and other explanations are more consistent with the scriptures. Among Abraham's family in Genesis, it is significant that *none* of the first sons received the birthright, and in each generation its recipient was determined by the Lord, not by the order of birth. Abraham's second son, Isaac, received precedence over the first, Ishmael, because God had promised that the son born to Sarah would be preeminent. Isaac's second son, Jacob, received the preeminence over the first, Esau, because the Lord wanted it that way and caused it to work out as he had foreordained. Joseph's selection over his brothers was also by divine designation, as was shown in his prophetic dreams. And the selection of Ephraim over Manasseh was the result of revelation to their grandfather Jacob (see Gen 48:9–20; Jer. 31:9).[3] Genesis does not hesitate to tell us that Joseph's mother,

Rachel, was the favorite of Jacob's four wives and that Joseph was his favorite son (see Gen. 29:30; 37:3). What we do not know from Genesis, however, is to what extent Jacob had prophetic reasons for his favoritism. Perhaps he knew before Joseph's birth—or even before his own marriages—that Rachel's son would have the greatest mission among his future children. Perhaps the "coat of many colors" was a sign of Joseph's birthright, which might explain his brothers' hostility concerning it.

The designation of "firstborn" in the Old Testament probably was important for the inheritance of property, although the biblical evidence is unclear.[4] But in a gospel context, the birthright has implications far beyond the inheritance of earthly goods. For us it represents the right of presidency, the keys to preside in the family through the Melchizedek Priesthood. Joseph's great-grandfather Abraham had sought the priesthood blessings that were his right through inheritance (see Abr. 1:2–4). Isaac received his birthright to preside in the family, after which Jacob was called. In the next generation, Joseph and his descendants were designated by revelation to preside in Israel. Latter-day Saints know by both observation and experience that to preside is to be in the service of others. Status and adulation are not the issues here, but leadership and sacrifice are the key components of the birthright designation.

Joseph's mother died when he was a young boy, and thus he probably was raised by one of his father's other wives among her own children. Certainly he was born in the covenant and was taught the gospel of Jesus Christ in his youth. That he chose imprisonment over fornication demonstrates that he knew what was right and wrong and had developed a strong and noble character as a young man. In Egypt, Joseph exercised tremendous spiritual gifts and prophetic powers. This, along with his background as a worthy son of Jacob, makes it reasonable to assume that he held the Melchizedek Priesthood before he went there.

Joseph's rise to power probably took place during Egypt's "Second Intermediate Period," when a dynasty of foreigners, the Hyksos, ruled the land (ca. 1664–1555 B.C.). The ancestors of the Hyksos were originally from Syria and Canaan and had migrated into the eastern Delta region in earlier centuries. During a time of internal weakness and chaos in Egypt, some of those immigrants seized control of the government and established a new line of kings. The Hyksos pharaohs used the Egyptian language, worshiped the Egyptian deities, and continued many of the political and social practices of their native Egyptian predecessors. When they in turn were overthrown by a powerful family from southern Egypt, the new pharaohs tried to remove all evidence of the Hyksos reign. This may explain why no trace of Joseph has been found in Egyptian inscriptions, and it probably explains the change in the status of the Israelites recorded at the beginning of Exodus: "Now there arose up a new king over Egypt, which knew not Joseph" (Ex. 1:8).

Genesis tells us that Pharaoh gave Joseph a wife named Asenath, whose name, "Belonging to (the goddess) Neith,"[5] indicates the devotion of her parents to their Egyptian religion. The Bible does not specify if the marriage took place at Joseph's request or if it was at the king's initiative. In either case the marriage showed that Joseph had ascended into the highest ranks of the Egyptian nobility, because Asenath's father was priest of the city of On (see Gen. 41:45, 50; 46:20). That city, better known as Heliopolis, was a center for the worship of the sun god Re.[6] Its priests came from prominent, influential families that probably had been in power long before the rise of the Hyksos rulers. In light of Asenath's family background, it seems unlikely that she was a believer in the true God when Joseph first met her. Yet it seems reasonable to conclude that in due time she became a convert to the gospel, was sealed for eternity with her husband, and reared her two sons, Manasseh and Ephraim, in the faith.[7]

"A SAVIOR UNTO MY PEOPLE"

The Book of Mormon restores an important prophecy from the biblical record of Joseph, presumably from the plates of brass. Moroni, the commander of the Nephite military, referred to a prophecy made by Jacob concerning the descendants of his son Joseph. Before his death Jacob saw that part of Joseph's coat had been preserved. He said: "Even as this remnant of garment of my son hath been preserved, so shall a remnant of the seed of my son be preserved by the hand of God, and be taken unto himself, while the remainder of the seed of Joseph shall perish, even as the remnant of his garment. Now behold, this giveth my soul sorrow; nevertheless, my soul hath joy in my son, because of that part of his seed which shall be taken unto God" (Alma 46:24–25). Latter-day Saints can see the fulfilment of Jacob's prophecy. Lehi's children, descendants of Joseph's son Manasseh, still live in their promised lands, and many thousands have been restored to the covenants of the gospel. Among those other descendants of Joseph who were scattered and lost among the nations in biblical times, many thousands, mostly from Ephraim, have now been brought back to the Church of Jesus Christ. God has preserved these remnants to perform an important mission for the rest of Israel and for all the world.

Before his death in Egypt, Jacob had Joseph bring his sons,

Manasseh and Ephraim, to receive blessings from their grandfather (see Gen. 48). Before the blessings were pronounced, Jacob told his son his intention to adopt the two boys as his own; they would be counted as his sons among the tribes of Israel. Hence the tribes included Manasseh and Ephraim, Israel's grandsons, while each of the other tribes was identified by the name of one of Israel's sons.

At Genesis 48:5 the Joseph Smith Translation inserts a significant expansion regarding Joseph's role in saving the family of Israel, and the role of his tribe in Israel's spiritual salvation in the latter days: "Therefore, O my son, he hath blessed me in raising thee up to be a servant unto me, in saving my house from death; in delivering my people, thy brethren, from famine which was sore in the land; wherefore the God of thy fathers shall bless thee, and the fruit of thy loins, that they shall be blessed above thy brethren, and above thy father's house; for thou hast prevailed, and thy father's house hath bowed down unto thee, even as it was shown unto thee, before thou wast sold into Egypt by the hands of thy brethren" (*I.V.* Gen. 48:8–10).

Joseph's life was a miracle. His birth to a mother who had been unable to conceive is identified in the Bible as an act of divine intervention (see Gen. 30:22–23). The circumstances by which he made his way into Egypt were miraculous. His brothers, with the worst of intent, had meant to do away with him because of their jealousy over his dreams of preeminence and over his special status with their father. Yet now those dreams had found fulfillment. Joseph was the ruler of Egypt to whom his brothers had bowed in solemn obeisance (see Gen. 42:6; see also vv. 7–9). Perhaps it was not until they arrived in Egypt that Joseph realized that it was God, not they, who had sent him there. By the time he revealed himself to them, he understood well that a divine hand had established him in Egypt to be their savior. As he told his brothers, "So now it was not you that sent me hither, but God" (Gen. 45:8). And "ye thought evil against me; but God meant it unto good, to bring to pass, as it is this day, to save much people alive" (Gen. 50:20). In a time of famine and economic despair, God saved the house of Israel from death by saving Joseph first, sending him in advance to Egypt, prospering him there, and then calling upon him to save the rest of the family.

Jacob's prophecy concerning Joseph looked forward to a later deliverance of which this earlier one was a foreshadowing: "Wherefore thy brethren shall bow down unto thee, from generation to generation, unto the fruit of thy loins for ever; for thou shalt be a light unto my people, to deliver them in the days of their captivity, from bondage; and to bring salvation unto them, when they are altogether bowed down under sin" (*I.V.* Gen. 48:10–11). According to this prophecy, the time would come in which Joseph's descendants would be a light to the house of Israel to deliver them from spiritual bondage. We see the fulfillment of this prophecy in the latter days. Joseph's two tribes, Ephraim and Manasseh, are the branches of Israel that are gathering first, just as ancient Joseph was made secure in Egypt before the coming of his brothers. Being safe within the covenants, it is now the calling of Joseph's descendants to gather the rest of the house of Israel to the blessings of the gospel. The bowing of the family members in his dreams thus ultimately represents their gratitude to his descendants for bearing the gospel to the family of Israel in the latter days.

Genesis 49 contains prophetic blessings that Jacob gave his twelve sons. Of these, the blessings and prophecies regarding Judah and Joseph are the most important and the longest. Joseph was promised blessings even greater than those of his ancestors: "The blessings of thy father have prevailed above the blessings of my progenitors unto the utmost bound of the everlasting hills: they shall be on the head of Joseph, and on the crown of the head of him that was separate from his brethren" (Gen. 49:26). Yet though the birthright was given to Joseph, the government of Israel would belong to Judah (see Gen. 49:10): "For Judah prevailed above his brethren, and of him came the chief ruler; but the birthright was Joseph's" (1 Chr. 5:2). In Israelite history God chose the tribe of Judah to govern until Christ, whose right it is to rule over his own kingdom (see Gen. 49:10). If the tribe of Ephraim led Israel in anything in Old Testament times, it was in wickedness. As the chief tribe of the northern kingdom after its separation from Judah, Ephraim was on the forefront of apostasy and idolatry and eventually guided the kingdom to destruction, deportation, and scattering. The birthright of Ephraim, it seems, would not be exercised in righteousness until the latter days, when God would raise up prophets from Ephraim who would restore their brethren to the covenants of the gospel. Like their ancestor Joseph who was sold into Egypt, the Ephraimites would prepare the way for the safe gathering of all the house of Israel, and they would preside among them in righteousness (see D&C 133:26–35). The Lord said to his birthright servants of Joseph in the latter days: "Ye are lawful heirs, according to the flesh, and have been hid from the world with Christ in God—therefore your life and the priesthood have remained. . . . Therefore, blessed are ye if ye continue in my goodness, a light unto the Gentiles, and through this priesthood, a savior unto my people Israel" (D&C 86:9–11). Joseph's mission in the latter days is to be not only a savior to the house of Israel but also "a light unto the Gentiles," the nations of the earth who are not descendants of Israel. In this also, the career of ancient Joseph was a type. His inspired work saved not only Israel but the Egyptians as well, by providing the means whereby they would live despite the severity of the famine. In our day of spiritual famine, when the nations of the world and the descendants of Israel alike are "altogether bowed down under sin" (*I.V.* Gen. 48:11), the mission of Joseph—embodied in the work of The Church of Jesus Christ of Latter-day Saints—is to save our brothers and sisters of Israel as well as our brothers and sisters of every nation. Indeed, "this gospel shall be preached unto every nation, and kindred, and tongue, and people" (D&C 133:37), because that is the mission of the children of Joseph in the latter days.

MOSES AND JOSEPH SMITH

A significant addition to Genesis in the Joseph Smith Translation is a lengthy expansion to the last three verses of the book. Genesis 50:24–26 is expanded dramatically in the New Translation, revealing a prophecy made by ancient Joseph concerning two great prophets who would be called to lead Israel in later generations—Moses and Joseph Smith.

Joseph prophesied to his people that they would be brought into bondage in Egypt but that God would provide a deliverer for them named Moses (*I.V.* Gen. 50:24–25, 29, 34–36).[8] He also foretold that they would be in bondage again later on, once again to be brought "out of darkness into light; out of hidden darkness." The latter-day deliverer would be a descendant of Joseph and would be named Joseph—like his esteemed ancestor and like his own father (*I.V.* Gen. 50:26–33). This great latter-day seer, clearly the Prophet Joseph Smith, would bring forth the word of the Lord to Israel, and he would convince them of the scriptures that they would already have. The descendants of Judah and the descendants of Joseph would each have scriptural records. Under the direction of the latter-day Joseph, those records would "grow together unto the confounding of false doctrines, and laying down of contentions, and establishing peace among the fruit of thy loins, and bringing them to a knowledge of their fathers in the latter days; and also to the knowledge of my covenants, saith the Lord" (I.V. Gen. 50:31).

Though this prophecy has not yet been fulfilled to its fullest extent, the process which it describes is well underway. The scriptures of Judah (the Old and New Testaments) have been brought together with the scriptures of Joseph (the Book of Mormon, the Doctrine and Covenants, and the Pearl of Great Price). The unified force of these great scriptures plays a powerful role in the establishment of the kingdom of God. It is significant that Joseph Smith's translation of Genesis 50 is quoted to a great extent in the Book of Mormon. The prophet Lehi found the revelation on the plates of brass and quoted much of it to his son, adding his prophecies concerning the future of his own people (see 2 Ne. 3). Joseph's last great prophecy, though lost or taken from the Bible in ancient times, survived on the plates of brass, the Old Testament of the family of Lehi (see 2 Ne. 4:2). It was restored anew in the last days from two sources—from Joseph Smith's New Translation of the Bible and from the record of Lehi in the Book of Mormon. As Nephi said of these prophecies of Joseph, "There are not many greater. And he prophesied concerning us, and our future generations" (2 Ne. 4:2).

NOTES

1. At Genesis 39:8 the Joseph Smith Translation changes "wotteth" to "knoweth," and at Genesis 39:22 the word "doer" is changed to "overseer."

At Genesis 44:15 "wot" is changed to "knew." Chapters 40–43 and 45–47 are marked "Correct" on the Joseph Smith Translation manuscript.

2. See Frederick E. Greenspahn, *When Brothers Dwell Together: The Preeminence of Younger Siblings in the Hebrew Bible* (New York and Oxford: Oxford University Press, 1994), 59–69.

3. In the Old Testament are several kings and other notables who were not firstborn sons but who succeeded their fathers by some other means of selection, probably through designation by the father. See Greenspahn, *When Brothers Dwell Together,* 74–81.

4. Greenspahn, *When Brothers Dwell Together,* 48–59.

5. Egyptian *Ns-nt;* Donald B. Redford, *A Study of the Biblical Story of Joseph (Genesis 37–50)* (Leiden: E. J. Brill, 1970), 229–30; J. Vergote, *Joseph en Égypte* (Louvain: Publications Universitaires, 1959), 148–50.

6. James P. Allen, "Heliopolis," *The Oxford Encyclopedia of Ancient Egypt,* ed. Donald B. Redford (Oxford: Oxford University Press, 2001), 2:88–89.

7. Writers who are uncomfortable with the idea of Joseph marrying an Egyptian have suggested that she, like the Hyksos rulers, was a descendant of immigrants from Syria-Canaan. This seems not only unlikely but also unnecessary.

8. Jewish texts from late antiquity preserve a tradition of Joseph prophesying about Moses. See John Tvedtnes, "Joseph's Prophecy of Moses and Aaron," *Insights* 21, no. 1 (2001): 2.

CONCLUSION

OF ALL THE BOOKS OF THE OLD and New Testaments, perhaps Genesis was in greater need of the Restoration than
any other. It may well be that the disproportionate amount of
modern revelation that affects Genesis indicates that it, more
than any other part of the Bible, suffered the kinds of losses
that were foreseen by Nephi (see 1 Ne. 13:23–30) and
described by Joseph Smith (see page 18, above). This should
not surprise us, however, because Genesis is the book that lays
the foundation for much biblical doctrine and biblical experience. Among its topics are the nature of the Godhead, the origin and character of Satan, the Creation, the Fall, the
Atonement, sacred record-keeping, ordinances, covenants,
curses, blessings, eternal families, prophets, promises, and chosen people. But "because of wickedness," as the scripture
teaches regarding one of these topics, these things are "not had
among the children of men" (Moses 1:23). Sadly, many of these
subjects are entirely absent from the pages of Genesis today.

The Restoration was not a candle lit in the darkness. It was
an explosion—an explosion that provided not only instant

brightness but also a sustained, continuous flood of illumination. It was not a blinding light but a light that opened eyes, gave sight to those who could not see, and led to ever-increasing vision. Because of what the Restoration does, Latter-day Saints must not—indeed *cannot*—read the Bible the way others read it. We cannot read Genesis without bringing to it our understanding of the nature of God, the atoning mission of Jesus Christ, the great plan for our happiness, the mission of covenant people, the eternal nature of family units, and a host of other truths that we learn through the Prophet Joseph Smith and the scriptures and doctrines he revealed. We give humble thanks for these things, and we rejoice that we are privileged to possess the knowledge made possible by the restored gospel.

SCRIPTURE INDEX

173

INDEX

Abel, 142

Abraham: saw Christ, 8; Genesis written for descendants of, 46; gave account of Creation, 68; gave tithes to Melchizedek, 119–20, 122; became father of great nation, 121, 128; received priesthood through Melchizedek, 123; as friend of God, 127; guided by Lord, 127; willingness of, to sacrifice all, 127–28, 129, 145, 150; as king, 128; descendants of, 132–36; as pattern, 136; and Sarah, 138–39; commanded to marry Hagar, 144; commanded to sacrifice Isaac, 144–45; intended victim of sacrifice, 145; king and priest to God, 145; has entered exaltation, 150; built altar, 153–54. *See also* Abraham, book of; Abrahamic covenant

Abraham, book of: account of Creation in, 56–57, 68, 69–74;

gives understanding of Abraham, Isaac, and Jacob, 138

Abrahamic covenant: promises of, 4, 129–36; as gospel of Jesus Christ, 128–29, 132, 135–36; circumcision a sign of, 141–43

Abram. *See* Abraham

Adam: creation of, 74, 77, 79–80, 82–84; before Fall, 76, 94; connection of, to earth, 83; meaning of name, 83; priesthood of, 85–86; and Fall, 90–95; responsibilities given to, 92; baptism of, 92; acted in our behalf, 95; after Fall, 92–93, 96–98; sins of posterity of, 101–2; gave posterity final blessing, 112

Adam-ondi-Ahman, 105, 112

Adoption, into house of Israel, 134–36

Adversity, 11

Affection, 102

Agency, 94, 95, 102

Allegory, 52

Alma, 95, 98, 122